"That Grand, Noble Work"

❖

Exploring the Constitution

A Resource Book

❖

Monticello

Produced by Knowledge Unlimited® Inc.
P.O. Box 52, Madison, WI 53701-0052
(800)356-2303 or (608)836-6660
www.ku.com

"That Grand, Noble Work" is copyright © 1998 by Knowledge Unlimited®, Inc., PO Box 52, Madison, Wisconsin, 53701. All rights reserved. **Teachers and group discussion leaders are hereby granted permission to reproduce any pages in this resource guide for classroom use only.** Otherwise, no parts of this book may be reproduced in any way without the expressed written permission of Knowledge Unlimited®, Inc. Printed in the U.S.A.

ISBN 1-55933-232-8

Table of Contents

Introduction & History 5
The Constitution of the United States 11
The Amendments 31
Activities for the Articles 47
Activities for the Amendments 71
Constitutional Timeline 105
Case Studies 109
Glossary 159

Using This Guide

"That Grand, Noble Work": Exploring the Constitution is a teacher's guide to the Constitution of the United States. It includes a historical introduction and the complete text of the Constitution and its amendments. The text is annotated so that students will be better able to understand what the parts of the Constitution call for. Following this, there are activities for both the articles and amendments, a timeline, a series of case studies, and a glossary.

This guide is designed for maximum flexibility. If your class works its way through all the sections here, students will come away with a much better understanding of the Constitution and why it is called a "living document." However, the lessons can be used independently of each other, so that you may focus on any of the parts of the Constitution you want.

The activities sections are designed to include the entire class in discussions and research. The activities include discussion questions, research/discussion questions, role plays, and essay questions. Most of these elements require some research on the part of students, but others do not. We encourage you to adapt any or all of these elements for your own use. For example, in many cases essay questions can also be used as class discussion questions, and vice versa. Suggested role plays can be adapted to your own special needs.

The timeline allows students to more easily visualize when in American history amendments were passed and when important Supreme Court decisions were made. Placing the amendments and cases in the context of American history will help students understand why certain amendments were written.

We have supplied 21 case studies, most of them based on actual cases the Supreme Court has heard. These studies call for students to make their own decisions about issues brought before the highest court in the land. (The actual decisions of the Supreme Court are printed after the case studies.) Finally, a glossary is provided of the most commonly-used constitutional terms.

The lessons and information in this book will help students appreciate what a "grand, noble work" the Constitution is — a work that continues to evolve as American society evolves.

Introduction & History

History of the Constitution

The Constitution of the United States is a document that spells out the basic rights of American citizens and sets down the rules for how to run the government. This document has guided our nation and guarded our freedoms for more than 200 years. But from the beginning, Americans have argued about many parts of the Constitution. As a result, some parts have been changed, and other parts now seem to have a different meaning than they used to.

Today, most Americans can hardly imagine life without the freedoms they enjoy. Yet without the Constitution, things would be very different in the United States.

Imagine a United States where the police could arrest you simply because you criticized the government. The right to speak or write down any idea, even ideas against the government, is one of the most important rights Americans hold. What if the police could open your mail without any good reason, without your permission, anytime they wanted? What if they could read anything that you had written or that somebody had written to you? What if you could be jailed for making a joke about the president?

Or suppose the government could take away your property without paying you anything for it? In America, your property is your own. Under special circumstances, such as when new roads or dams are built, the federal, state, or local government can tear down your home and make you move — but that government must pay you for your loss.

We sometimes read about the military in another country taking over the nation's capitol and installing a new government. The United States has never been seriously threatened in this manner — and most experts agree that's because the Constitution has acted to make our nation stable. We take for granted that we will elect our leaders and that our decisions will be respected. But what would happen if we didn't have the stable form of government called for in the Constitution?

The Constitution begins with these words: "We the People of the United States, in order to form a more perfect union . . . do ordain and establish this Constitution." It is one of the most famous and important documents ever written, and it has helped make the U.S. one of the most democratic nations on Earth.

The U.S. won its independence from Great Britain in 1781. But by 1787, many American leaders — including George Washington, Benjamin Franklin, and James Madison — were worried that the new nation might not last. The nation was ruled at the time by the Articles of Confederation, which gave most governing powers to the states. There was a U.S. Congress, which had the power to make new states and to declare war on other nations. But there was no president and no Supreme Court. Many people in the United States liked it this way. They were Anti-Federalists — that is, they opposed a strong national government and favored strong state governments.

It soon became clear that as a nation, the United States wasn't working. Under the Articles, each state had its own currency, and each state made its own rules about trade. Many states set up special taxes called tariffs on goods from other states. This made it hard for each state to trade with others. Bitter arguments among the states became increasingly common.

In the 1780s, farmers across the new nation were having a hard time earning money. Many faced imprisonment because they could not pay their debts. Others faced the loss of their farms. Some farmers in Massachusetts asked the state government for help. The government turned them down. Then, about 1,000 farmers led by Daniel Shays, a Revolutionary War soldier, took up arms and began forcing the state's courts to close.

The national government was unable to stop the uprising. Eventually, the Massachusetts militia was able to put an end to Shays's Rebellion, as it has come to be known. The rebellion led many people to call for the revision of the Articles of Confederation. Specifically, people wanted to see a stronger central government.

So, in May of 1787, George Washington called for a constitutional convention in Philadelphia, Pennsylvania. With Washington guiding their discussions, the delegates at the convention took four months to complete their task. When they were done, they had created a blueprint for running a federal system — a strong and free government that splits powers between the national and state governments.

The Constitution divides the national government into three branches. Congress is the legislative branch, which means it makes the laws for the United States. Congress is split into two parts: the Senate and the House of Representatives. The executive branch, which is headed by the president, carries out the laws Congress makes. The third branch of government, the judicial branch, is the system of federal courts in the U.S. The most powerful of these is the Supreme Court. The judicial branch makes sure the laws that are made are obeyed, interprets what these laws mean, and has the power to overturn laws if they go against the Constitution.

The Constitution gives the national government a great deal of power. But other important rules in the Constitution describe things the government is not allowed to do. There are several rules setting limits on the government that help to protect the rights of citizens.

Each branch of the national government keeps the others from becoming too powerful. This system is called "checks and balances." For example, one way the executive branch balances the legislative branch is when the president vetoes, or blocks, laws passed by Congress. In turn, Congress has the power to approve advisers and other government officials chosen by the president before these officials can take their jobs. Federal courts and the U.S. Supreme Court balance the other two branches by deciding if any law goes against the Constitution or if a law is being unfairly enforced. These are just some of the ways the three branches of government check one another's power. This system is spelled out in the Constitution.

The Constitution helps protect the rights of ordinary citizens by setting limits on the power of the national government. In many countries, government leaders have much more power over ordinary citizens than do leaders in the U.S. For example, they might be able to put people in jail for no reason, and no one can stop them. In these countries, people often must fight to win the rights Americans take for granted.

But the Constitution alone does not describe all the rights we have today. Years after the Constitution was signed, many important rights still were not included in it. They had to be added to the Constitution later. And not all Americans were able to share in the rights that did exist. For many years after 1787, neither women nor black people were allowed to vote. After the Civil War, when all men should have been allowed to vote freely, some states passed laws designed to keep former slaves and their families from participating in elections. Women did not get the right to vote until 1920. And laws in several states allowed officials to shut down newspapers they didn't like.

People have disagreed about the meanings of different parts of the Constitution from the beginning. The issue of whether the Constitution gives the government too much power is one argument that has raged since 1787. Other disagreements have focused on language in the document that some find vague and confusing.

When there are disagreements over how to interpret the Constitution, it is up to the federal courts and the Supreme Court to decide them. The Supreme Court is made up of nine judges, called justices, who can serve for life once they are appointed by the president and approved by Congress. These nine justices and other federal judges in the U.S. hear cases brought before them and make decisions about whether other judges have followed the Constitution in their rulings.

Supreme Court decisions change how we view what the Constitution says. The Supreme Court is very important because it explains what the framers of the Constitution meant 200 years ago and shows judges in lower courts how they should rule. This affects everyone in the country. Of course, there were only four million people in the U.S. in 1787, and most of them were farmers. Things have changed a great deal in our nation since then. That is one of the reasons there are so many arguments about how the Constitution applies to our lives today.

The Supreme Court's power to interpret the Constitution is not entirely spelled out in the Constitution itself. It was not until 1801, when John Marshall became the chief justice of the Supreme Court, that the Court began to assume a leading role in government. Marshall began to clarify the Court's power by establishing the principle of "judicial review." Judicial review refers to the right of federal courts — but especially the Supreme Court — to disallow any act or law made by the federal or state government that is found to go against the Constitution.

In exercising judicial review, the Supreme Court has to interpret or explain or even reinterpret various phrases in the Constitution. Over the years, the justices of the Supreme Court have disagreed about how much they should interpret the Constitution. This argument — both in and outside the Court — often takes the form of disputes between so-called loose constructionists and strict constructionists. A "loose constructionist" tends to interpret the phrases of the Constitution broadly, applying them to a wide variety of problems. A loose constructionist believes that the Constitution is a living, changing, document that must keep up with modern times. A "strict constructionist" believes that the Court's interpretations should be limited only to what the Constitution's phrases themselves say or imply.

Sometimes the justices of the Supreme Court even reverse themselves — that is, they reverse a past decision of the Court. One of the most famous examples of this occurred in 1954, when the court decided the case of *Brown v. Board of Education*, which reversed the policy of "separate but equal" facilities for blacks and whites in schools and other public places. The doctrine of "separate but equal" had been approved by the court in 1896, in the case of *Plessy v. Ferguson*.

The Constitution has been amended, or changed, 27 times since it was written. Amendments have usually come in response to changing ways of thinking about how we live our lives. One example of this change occurred in 1865, when Congress passed the 13th Amendment, which ended the practice of slavery in all parts of the United States. Another example is the 22nd Amendment. After Franklin Delano Roosevelt was elected president four times in a row, Congress passed the 22nd Amendment, which says that no one can be elected president more than twice.

Another big disagreement about the Constitution centers on the question of whether the national government or the state governments should be more powerful. The original 13 states felt very strongly that their rights should be protected. But are they protected enough?

The most tragic argument about this question led to the Civil War. The Civil War, which lasted from 1861 to 1865, was largely about the issue of slavery. But it started over the issue of states' rights. The southern states said the national government had no right to make laws against slavery in any part of the country. They said only a state could make laws regarding issues within its own borders — that power had been given to the states by the Constitution. The southern states even felt that if a settlement on this matter couldn't be reached with northern states, the southern states could secede, or separate, from the rest of the United States and form their own country. The southern states said they could ignore any federal law they felt was unconstitutional. The U.S. government, led by Abraham Lincoln, said the national government had the right to make laws for the entire nation. The U.S. government denied that the southern states had the right to secede, and the Civil War began. When the U.S. Army defeated the southern Confederate Army, the issue was resolved in favor of the national government and against the idea of states seceding from the Union.

The question of the rights of individual citizens has been an important one as well. Many of the Constitution's framers felt the original Constitution did not do enough to guarantee people's freedoms. Very soon after the Constitution was put into effect, Congress passed its first ten amendments, which are called the Bill of Rights. These guaranteed freedom of speech and of the press, freedom of religion, the right to a fair trial, and the right to keep one's property and not have it taken away unfairly.

However, these ten amendments at first seemed only to apply to the federal government and not to state governments. For a long time, the Supreme Court chose to rule that state governments were not bound by the Bill of Rights and were free to make any decisions they saw fit. Even after the 14th Amendment was passed saying that no state could "deprive any person of life, liberty, or property without due process of law," the Supreme Court refused to hold state governments to the Bill of Rights. This refusal applied to many different areas of life, from business and child labor laws to voting rights and the right to a fair trial. Finally, in 1931, the Supreme Court ruled that a state could not restrict the free speech of any individual. Other parts of the Bill of Rights now apply to every American, but to this day states do not have to follow all parts of the Bill of Rights.

It's important to remember that the Constitution is just a piece of paper unless governments and people put its statements into practice. Many of the writers of the Constitution, for example, owned slaves, and slaves were not given any of the rights guaranteed in the Constitution. Even after the Civil War many states passed laws that legalized the unequal treatment of African Americans and others. These examples, and many more, have made some people doubt whether the Constitution is strong enough to keep states from taking away the rights of Americans even today.

For many, the most important questions center on what courts should do about rights not mentioned in the Constitution. For example, Congress in the eighteenth century had no way of predicting the use of telephones, or the wiretapping of telephones, when it wrote in the Fourth Amendment that "the right of the people to be secure . . . against unreasonable searches and seizures, shall not be violated." However, in 1918, a man took a case to the Supreme Court saying that his Fourth Amendment rights had been violated because his phone was tapped. In cases like this, the Supreme Court justices must apply what they think the framers meant in the Constitution to today's situations and make their ruling accordingly.

The Constitution is a living document because we are always working on what it means and rethinking the Supreme Court's decisions. It is in this way that the U.S. operates on the same principles now that it did more than 200 years ago, even through huge changes in the American way of life. New challenges will always come up, and the constitutional system is designed to deal with them when they do.

Constitution of the United States of America

NOTE TO TEACHER

The articles of the Constitution set out in some detail how the government of the United States is to be run. The first three articles explain the duties of the legislative, executive, and judicial branches of the federal government. Article IV addresses the government's relations to the states and the states' relations to each other. The final three articles detail how to amend the Constitution, state that the Constitution and other federal laws outrank state laws, and provide for the ratification of the document.

Considering their length and age, these articles have been amended very few times. When a part of the articles has been amended or changed through legislation, we have placed brackets [ ] around the section.

Before and after each section, we have also written an explanation, or breakdown, of what the section provides for. We encourage you to copy the articles for your class for use later in the activities section.

The Constitution of the United States of America

Preamble

> We the people of the United States, in order to form a more perfect union, establish justice, insure domestic tranquility, provide for the common defense, promote the general welfare, and secure the blessings of liberty to ourselves and our posterity, do ordain and establish this Constitution for the United States of America.

The Preamble to the Constitution
- States that the government of the United States will be of the people and not of the states — that is, the people's interests outweigh the states'.
- Says the Constitution was written to "form a more perfect union" — that is, it replaces the Articles of Confederation, which had been in effect since 1781 when the United States became independent from Great Britain.

Article I

The first article of the Constitution outlines the power of the legislative branch of the federal government — that is, Congress. It lists the requirements for serving in Congress, tells us how the body is organized, and explains its powers. It also describes which powers are forbidden to Congress and the states.

Section 1.

> All legislative powers herein granted shall be vested in a Congress of the United States, which shall consist of a Senate and House of Representatives.

This section states that there will be two parts of Congress, a Senate and a House of Representatives.

Section 2.

> The House of Representatives shall be composed of members chosen every second year by the people of the several states, and the electors in each state shall have the qualifications requisite for electors of the most numerous branch of the state legislature.

continued on next page

> *continued from previous page*
>
> No person shall be a representative who shall not have attained to the age of twenty five years, and been seven years a citizen of the United States, and who shall not, when elected, be an inhabitant of that state in which he shall be chosen.
>
> [Representatives and direct taxes shall be apportioned among the several states which may be included within this union, according to their respective numbers, which shall be determined by adding to the whole number of free persons, including those bound to service for a term of years, and excluding Indians not taxed, three fifths of all other persons. The actual enumeration shall be made within three years after the first meeting of the Congress of the United States, and within every subsequent term of ten years, in such manner as they shall by law direct. The number of representatives shall not exceed one for every thirty thousand, but each state shall have at least one representative; and until such enumeration shall be made, the state of New Hampshire shall be entitled to chuse three, Massachusetts eight, Rhode Island and Providence Plantations one, Connecticut five, New York six, New Jersey four, Pennsylvania eight, Delaware one, Maryland six, Virginia ten, North Carolina five, South Carolina five, and Georgia three.]
>
> When vacancies happen in the Representation from any state, the executive authority thereof shall issue writs of election to fill such vacancies.
>
> The House of representatives shall choose their speaker and other officers; and shall have the sole power of impeachment.

This section

- Provides for the popular election of members to the House of Representatives and leaves it up to each state to decide who can vote.

- Requires that a representative must be at least 25 years old, a citizen of the U.S. for seven years, and a resident of the state in which he or she is elected.

- Provides that the number of representatives given to each state be based on population, with each state having at least one member in the House.

- Provides for a census of the U.S. population, which must be taken every ten years.

- [The effect of this section has been greatly changed since it was written:
Direct taxes probably refers to poll taxes and property taxes. Poll taxes were made unconstitutional by the 24th Amendment. The 16th Amendment allowed Congress to impose an income tax on individuals, rather than to tax a person according to the population of his or her state.

   The other persons referred to in "three-fifths of all other persons" meant slaves. The Civil War and the 13th Amendment abolished slavery and made this section obsolete.

   There is no longer a requirement that there "shall be no more than one representative for every 30,000 people." The size of the House was fixed at 435 members in 1929. Each member of the House represents approximately 540,000 people.]

- States that if a vacancy occurs in the House, the state governor must call a special election.
- Gives the House the power to pick its own leaders.
- States that the House alone has the power to impeach, or accuse, a high government official of a crime.

Section 3.

> The Senate of the United States shall be composed of two senators from each state, [chosen by the legislature thereof,] for six years; and each senator shall have one vote.
>
> Immediately after they shall be assembled in consequence of the first election, they shall be divided as equally as may be into three classes. The seats of the senators of the first class shall be vacated at the expiration of the second year, of the second class at the expiration of the fourth year, and the third class at the expiration of the sixth year, so that one third may be chosen every second year; and if vacancies happen by resignation, or otherwise, during the recess of the legislature of any state, the executive thereof may make temporary appointments [until the next meeting of the legislature, which shall then fill such vacancies].
>
> No person shall be a senator who shall not have attained to the age of thirty years, and been nine years a citizen of the United States and who shall not, when elected, be an inhabitant of that state for which he shall be chosen.
>
> The Vice President of the United States shall be president of the senate, but shall have no vote, unless they be equally divided.
>
> The Senate shall choose their other officers, and also a president pro tempore, in the absence of the Vice President, or when he shall exercise the office of President of the United States.
>
> The Senate shall have the sole power to try all impeachments. When sitting for that purpose, they shall be on oath or affirmation. When the President of the United States is tried, the chief justice shall preside: And no person shall be convicted without the concurrence of two thirds of the members present.
>
> Judgment in cases of impeachment shall not extend further than to removal from office, and disqualification to hold and enjoy any office of honor, trust or profit under the United States: but the party convicted shall nevertheless be liable and subject to indictment, trial, judgment and punishment, according to law.

This section

- Declares that each state in the United States will have two senators and that a Senate term is six years.
- [The 17th Amendment provides that senators are to be elected by the people in their states, not appointed by state legislatures.]
- States that one-third of the Senate must be elected every two years.
- Requires a senator to be at least 30 years old, a citizen of the United States for nine years, and a resident of the state he or she represents.
- Makes the vice president the president of the Senate but doesn't give the vice president a vote unless there is a tie.
- Allows the Senate to choose a president pro tempore, or someone to fill the vice president's spot if the vice president is absent.
- Empowers the Senate to try impeachments and requires senators to swear an oath before any trial, just as jurors in a regular trial must do. A two-thirds vote is necessary to convict someone in an impeachment trial. The Senate can only remove an official from office, but the person removed also can be tried in a regular court.

Section 4.

> The times, places and manner of holding elections for senators and representatives, shall be prescribed in each state by the legislature thereof; but the Congress may at any time by law make or alter such regulations, [except as to the places of choosing senators.]
>
> The Congress shall assemble at least once in every year, [and such meeting shall be on the first Monday in December,] unless they shall by law appoint a different day.

This section

- Gives state legislatures the power to dictate when, where, and how senators are chosen for office. Congress, however, can alter these regulations.
- [The 17th Amendment set aside, or made obsolete, the words bracketed in the first paragraph of Section 4. The paragraph prevents Congress from fixing the "place of choosing" of senators by the state legislature, because that would have given Congress the power to tell each state where to locate its capital.]
- Requires Congress to meet at least once a year.
- [This part of the second paragraph was set aside by the 20th Amendment, which changed the date to January 3.]

Section 5.

> Each house shall be the judge of the elections, returns and qualifications of its own members, and a majority of each shall constitute a quorum to do business; but a smaller number may adjourn from day to day, and may be authorized to compel the attendance of absent members, in such manner, and under such penalties as each house may provide.
>
> Each house may determine the rules of its proceedings, punish its members for disorderly behavior, and, with the concurrence of two thirds, expel a member.
>
> Each house shall keep a journal of its proceedings, and from time to time publish the same, excepting such parts as may in their judgment require secrecy; and the yeas and nays of the members of either house on any question shall, at the desire of one fifth of those present, be entered on the journal.
>
> Neither house, during the session of Congress, shall, without the consent of the other, adjourn for more than three days, nor to any other place than that in which the two houses shall be sitting.

This section

- Gives each part of Congress the power to judge the election and qualifications of its members.
- Says that in order to do business, each part of Congress must have a quorum. In this case, a quorum is a majority of the members of each house in Congress — 26 senators and 218 representatives.
- Gives each part of Congress the right to set its own rules as to how its body will be run.
- Requires each part of Congress to keep a record of its proceedings and publish it.
- Says that neither part of Congress can adjourn for more than three days while Congress is in session without the permission of the other part of Congress.

Section 6.

> The senators and representatives shall receive a compensation for their services, to be ascertained by law, and paid out of the treasury of the United States. They shall in all cases, except treason, felony and breach of the peace, be privileged from arrest during their attendance at the session of their respective houses, and in going to and returning from the same; and for any speech or debate in either house, they shall not be questioned in any other place.
>
> No senator or representative shall, during the time for which he was elected, be appointed to any civil office under the authority of the United States, which shall have been created, or the emoluments whereof shall have been increased during

— continued on next page —

> *continued from previous page*
>
> such time: and no person holding any office under the United States, shall be a member of either house during his continuance in office.

This section

- Provides for paying the members of Congress.

- Says that while Congress is in session, a member cannot be arrested or sued, except in cases of treason and felony.

- Allows members of Congress to say anything on the floor of the House or Senate and not be sued for it.

- Forbids the appointment of members of Congress to any job outside of Congress that Congress helped create.

- Forbids anyone who holds another office in government to also hold a seat in Congress.

Section 7.

> All bills for raising revenue shall originate in the House of Representatives; but the Senate may propose or concur with amendments as on other bills.
>
> Every bill which shall have passed the House of Representatives and the Senate, shall, before it become a law, be presented to the President of the United States; if he approve he shall sign it, but if not he shall return it, with his objections to that house in which it shall have originated, who shall enter the objections at large on their journal, and proceed to reconsider it. If after such reconsideration two thirds of that house shall agree to pass the bill, it shall be sent, together with the objections, to the other house, by which it shall likewise be reconsidered, and if approved by two thirds of that house, it shall become a law. But in all such cases the votes of both houses shall be determined by yeas and nays, and the names of the persons voting for and against the bill shall be entered on the journal of each house respectively. If any bill shall not be returned by the President within ten days (Sundays excepted) after it shall have been presented to him, the same shall be a law, in like manner as if he had signed it, unless the Congress by their adjournment prevent its return, in which case it shall not be a law.
>
> Every order, resolution, or vote to which the concurrence of the Senate and House of Representatives may be necessary (except on a question of adjournment) shall be presented to the President of the United States; and before the same shall take effect, shall be approved by him, or being disapproved by him, shall be repassed by two thirds of the Senate and House of Representatives, according to the rules and limitations prescribed in the case of a bill.

This section
- Gives the House of Representatives the duty to originate all tax bills, but gives the Senate the power to revise the House's proposals.

- Requires that a bill must pass both houses of Congress in order to become a law.
- Requires that a bill passed by Congress must go to the president for his or her signature.
- Gives the president the power to veto, or reject, a bill, and send it back to Congress.
- States that if a bill is passed and is not vetoed within 10 days by the president, it becomes a law — unless Congress adjourns before the president can veto the bill.
- Gives Congress the power to overturn the president's veto by a two-thirds vote in each house.

Section 8.

The Congress shall have power to lay and collect taxes, duties, imposts and excises, to pay the debts and provide for the common defense and general welfare of the United States; but all duties, imposts and excises shall be uniform throughout the United States;

To borrow money on the credit of the United States;

To regulate commerce with foreign nations, and among the several states, and with the Indian tribes;

To establish a uniform rule of naturalization, and uniform laws on the subject of bankruptcies throughout the United States;

To coin money, regulate the value thereof, and of foreign coin, and fix the standard of weights and measures;

To provide for the punishment of counterfeiting the securities and current coin of the United States;

To establish post offices and post roads;

To promote the progress of science and useful arts, by securing for limited times to authors and inventors the exclusive right to their respective writings and discoveries;

To constitute tribunals inferior to the Supreme Court;

To define and punish piracies and felonies committed on the high seas, and offenses against the law of nations;

To declare war, grant letters of marque and reprisal, and make rules concerning captures on land and water;

To raise and support armies, but no appropriation of money to that use shall be for a longer term than two years;

— continued on next page —

> *continued from previous page*
>
> To provide and maintain a navy;
>
> To make rules for the government and regulation of the land and naval forces;
>
> To provide for calling forth the militia to execute the laws of the union, suppress insurrections and repel invasions;
>
> To provide for organizing, arming, and disciplining, the militia, and for governing such part of them as may be employed in the service of the United States, reserving to the states respectively, the appointment of the officers, and the authority of training the militia according to the discipline prescribed by Congress;
>
> To exercise exclusive legislation in all cases whatsoever, over such District (not exceeding ten miles square) as may, by cession of particular states, and the acceptance of Congress, become the seat of the government of the United States, and to exercise like authority over all places purchased by the consent of the legislature of the state in which the same shall be, for the erection of forts, magazines, arsenals, dockyards, and other needful buildings; —And
>
> To make all laws which shall be necessary and proper for carrying into execution the foregoing powers, and all other powers vested by this Constitution in the government of the United States, or in any department or officer thereof.

This section outlines the powers of Congress, including the right to put forth taxes, regulate commerce, set rules for naturalization of immigrants, establish courts less powerful than the Supreme Court, declare war, raise and support an army and navy, and make all the laws for the federal government.

Section 9.

> The migration or importation of such persons as any of the states now existing shall think proper to admit, shall not be prohibited by the Congress prior to the year one thousand eight hundred and eight, but a tax or duty may be imposed on such importation, not exceeding ten dollars for each person.
>
> The privilege of the writ of habeas corpus shall not be suspended, unless when in cases of rebellion or invasion the public safety may require it.
>
> No bill of attainder or ex post facto law shall be passed.
>
> No capitation, [or other direct,] tax shall be laid, unless in proportion to the census or enumeration herein before directed to be taken.
>
> No tax or duty shall be laid on articles exported from any state.
>
> No preference shall be given by any regulation of commerce or revenue to the
>
> *continued on next page*

> *continued from previous page*
>
> ports of one state over those of another: nor shall vessels bound to, or from, one state, be obliged to enter, clear or pay duties in another.
>
> No money shall be drawn from the treasury, but in consequence of appropriations made by law; and a regular statement and account of receipts and expenditures of all public money shall be published from time to time.
>
> No title of nobility shall be granted by the United States: and no person holding any office of profit or trust under them, shall, without the consent of the Congress, accept of any present, emolument, office, or title, of any kind whatever, from any king, prince, or foreign state.

This section outlines the powers Congress does not have

- The first section keeps Congress from banning the importation of slaves into the United States before 1808.
- Congress cannot pass a bill of attainder, or an act that punishes a person without a trial. It cannot pass an ex post facto law, or a law that makes an act a crime aimed at prosecuting persons who committed the act when it was not a crime.
- Congress cannot pass a capitation — or head tax — or poll tax or other direct taxes on everyone. [The words "or other direct" were set aside by the 16th Amendment, which allows Congress to levy an income tax on citizens.]
- Congress cannot tax shipments from one state to another or favor one state over another in trade and commerce.
- Government money cannot be spent without the consent of Congress, and Congress must account for the money it spends.
- Congress cannot give anyone a title of nobility.

Section 10.

> No state shall enter into any treaty, alliance, or confederation; grant letters of marque and reprisal; coin money; emit bills of credit; make anything but gold and silver coin a tender in payment of debts; pass any bill of attainder, ex post facto law, or law impairing the obligation of contracts, or grant any title of nobility.
>
> No state shall, without the consent of the Congress, lay any imposts or duties on imports or exports, except what may be absolutely necessary for executing its inspection laws: and the net produce of all duties and imposts, laid by any state on imports or exports, shall be for the use of the treasury of the United States; and all such laws shall be subject to the revision and control of the Congress.
>
> No state shall, without the consent of Congress, lay any duty of tonnage, keep troops, or ships of war in time of peace, enter into any agreement or compact with another state, or with a foreign power, or engage in war, unless actually invaded, or in such imminent danger as will not admit of delay.

This section limits the powers of the states. States cannot tax goods coming into or leaving their borders without the consent of Congress. States cannot make treaties with other nations, or declare war on them.

Article II

The second article defines the executive branch of government — that is, the presidency. It sets rules about how the president is elected, lists the qualifications for the presidency and defines the president's powers.

Section 1.

The executive power shall be vested in a President of the United States of America. He shall hold his office during the term of four years, and, together with the Vice President, chosen for the same term, be elected, as follows:

Each state shall appoint, in such manner as the legislature thereof may direct, a number of electors, equal to the whole number of senators and representatives to which the state may be entitled in the Congress: but no senator or representative, or person holding an office of trust or profit under the United States, shall be appointed an elector.

[The electors shall meet in their respective states, and vote by ballot for two persons, of whom one at least shall not be an inhabitant of the same state with themselves. And they shall make a list of all the persons voted for, and of the number of votes for each; which list they shall sign and certify, and transmit sealed to the seat of the government of the United States, directed to the president of the Senate. The president of the Senate shall, in the presence of the Senate and House of Representatives, open all the certificates, and the votes shall then be counted. The person having the greatest number of votes shall be the President, if such number be a majority of the whole number of electors appointed; and if there be more than one who have such majority, and have an equal number of votes, then the House of Representatives shall immediately choose by ballot one of them for President; and if no person have a majority, then from the five highest on the list the said House shall in like manner choose the President. But in choosing the President, the votes shall be taken by states, the representation from each state having one vote; A quorum for this purpose shall consist of a member or members from two thirds of the states, and a majority of all the states shall be necessary to a choice. In every case, after the choice of the President, the person having the greatest number of votes of the electors shall be the Vice President. But if there should remain two or more who have equal votes, the Senate shall choose from them by ballot the Vice President.]

The Congress may determine the time of choosing the electors, and the day on which they shall give their votes; which day shall be the same throughout the United States.

continued on next page

> *continued from previous page*
>
> No person except a natural born citizen, or a citizen of the United States, at the time of the adoption of this Constitution, shall be eligible to the office of President; neither shall any person be eligible to that office who shall not have attained to the age of thirty five years, and been fourteen years a resident within the United States.
>
> In case of the removal of the President from office, or of his death, resignation, or inability to discharge the powers and duties of the said office, the same shall devolve on the Vice President, and the Congress may by law provide for the case of removal, death, resignation or inability, both of the President and Vice President, declaring what officer shall then act as President, and such officer shall act accordingly, until the disability be removed, or a President shall be elected.
>
> The President shall, at stated times, receive for his services, a compensation, which shall neither be increased nor diminished during the period for which he shall have been elected, and he shall not receive within that period any other emolument from the United States, or any of them.
>
> Before he enter on the execution of his office, he shall take the following oath or affirmation: — "I do solemnly swear (or affirm) that I will faithfully execute the office of President of the United States, and will to the best of my ability, preserve, protect and defend the Constitution of the United States."

This section
- Establishes the Electoral College, a group of people elected by the voters in each state to elect the president and vice president.
- [Establishes how presidents are chosen by the House of Representatives in case no candidate wins a majority of the electoral vote. This procedure was changed by the 12th Amendment.]
- Requires that a president must be born a U.S. citizen, must be at least 35 years old, and must have lived in the United States for 14 years.
- States that the president must be paid and that during his or her time in office the pay can't be increased or decreased.
- Requires the president to take an oath of office as written in this section.

Section 2.

> The President shall be commander in chief of the Army and Navy of the United States, and of the militia of the several states, when called into the actual service of the United States; he may require the opinion, in writing, of the principal officer in each of the executive departments, upon any subject relating to the duties of their respective offices, and he shall have power to grant reprieves and pardons for offenses against the United States, except in cases of impeachment.
>
> *continued on next page*

> *continued from previous page*
>
> He shall have power, by and with the advice and consent of the Senate, to make treaties, provided two thirds of the senators present concur; and he shall nominate, and by and with the advice and consent of the Senate, shall appoint ambassadors, other public ministers and consuls, judges of the Supreme Court, and all other officers of the United States, whose appointments are not herein otherwise provided for, and which shall be established by law: but the Congress may by law vest the appointment of such inferior officers, as they think proper, in the President alone, in the courts of law, or in the heads of departments.
>
> The President shall have power to fill up all vacancies that may happen during the recess of the Senate, by granting commissions which shall expire at the end of their next session.

This section
- Makes the president the commander-in-chief of the military and of the state militias, or the National Guard.
- Allows the president to make various appointments, many of them with the approval of the Senate.

Section 3.

> He shall from time to time give to the Congress information of the state of the union, and recommend to their consideration such measures as he shall judge necessary and expedient; he may, on extraordinary occasions, convene both houses, or either of them, and in case of disagreement between them, with respect to the time of adjournment, he may adjourn them to such time as he shall think proper; he shall receive ambassadors and other public ministers; he shall take care that the laws be faithfully executed, and shall commission all the officers of the United States.

This section
- Requires the president to give information about the state of the nation to Congress "from time to time."
- Gives the president the power to call Congress into session and the power to adjourn Congress, if events warrant it.
- Makes it the president's duty to receive foreign officials.
- Gives the president the power to commission all military officers.
- Requires the president to make sure laws are followed.

Section 4.

> The President, Vice President and all civil officers of the United States, shall be removed from office on impeachment for, and conviction of, treason, bribery, or other high crimes and misdemeanors.

This section provides for the impeachment, or trial for removal from office, of the president and other high government officials.

Article III

The third article outlines the duties and powers of the judicial branch of government. The judicial branch is made up of the Supreme Court and inferior courts. "Inferior" here means any court that is not as high as the Supreme Court.

Section 1.

> The judicial power of the United States, shall be vested in one Supreme Court, and in such inferior courts as the Congress may from time to time ordain and establish. The judges, both of the supreme and inferior courts, shall hold their offices during good behaviour, and shall, at stated times, receive for their services, a compensation, which shall not be diminished during their continuance in office.

This section
- Establishes a Supreme Court and inferior courts.
- Gives Congress the power to establish the number of inferior courts it thinks is necessary.
- Says that justices and judges can hold their positions for as long as they want, unless they are impeached and removed from office.
- Says that justices and judges will be paid.

Section 2.

> The judicial power shall extend to all cases, in law and equity, arising under this Constitution, the laws of the United States, and treaties made, or which shall be made, under their authority;—to all cases affecting ambassadors, other public ministers and consuls;—to all cases of admiralty and maritime jurisdiction;—to controversies to which the United States shall be a party;—to controversies between two or more states; [—between a state and citizens of another state;] — between citizens of different states; — between citizens of the same state claiming lands under grants of different states, and between a state, or the citizens thereof, and foreign states, citizens or subjects.

— continued on next page —

> *continued from previous page*
>
> In all cases affecting ambassadors, other public ministers and consuls, and those in which a state shall be party, the Supreme Court shall have original jurisdiction. In all the other cases before mentioned, the Supreme Court shall have appellate jurisdiction, both as to law and fact, with such exceptions, and under such regulations as the Congress shall make.
>
> The trial of all crimes, except in cases of impeachment, shall be by jury; and such trial shall be held in the state where the said crimes shall have been committed; but when not committed within any state, the trial shall be at such place or places as the Congress may by law have directed.

This section
- Gives the Supreme Court the power to declare the laws of Congress unconstitutional.
- Outlines the jurisdiction — the duties, powers, and even territories — of the Supreme Court and inferior courts. [The words "between a state and citizens of another state" were set aside by the 11th Amendment.]
- Says that the Supreme Court is an appellate, or appeals, court, except if a case involves high public officials or a state. In that event, the case goes immediately to the Supreme Court for judgment.
- Says that trials will be heard before juries and in the state where the crimes were committed.

Section 3.

> Treason against the United States, shall consist only in levying war against them, or in adhering to their enemies, giving them aid and comfort. No person shall be convicted of treason unless on the testimony of two witnesses to the same overt act, or on confession in open court.
>
> The Congress shall have power to declare the punishment of treason, but no attainder of treason shall work corruption of blood, or forfeiture except during the life of the person attainted.

This section
- Defines treason and says that no person can be convicted of treason without a confession or the testimony of at least two witnesses.
- Says that the families of people convicted of treason do not share their guilt.

Article IV

This article deals with the relations of states to each other and of the federal government to the states. Much of this article was taken directly from the Articles of Confederation, the document the Constitution replaced.

Section 1.

> Full faith and credit shall be given in each state to the public acts, records, and judicial proceedings of every other state. And the Congress may by general laws prescribe the manner in which such acts, records, and proceedings shall be proved, and the effect thereof.

This section says that states must respect the laws of other states. Congress can oversee the relationships of the states.

Section 2.

> The citizens of each state shall be entitled to all privileges and immunities of citizens in the several states.
>
> A person charged in any state with treason, felony, or other crime, who shall flee from justice, and be found in another state, shall on demand of the executive authority of the state from which he fled, be delivered up, to be removed to the state having jurisdiction of the crime.
>
> [No person held to service or labor in one state, under the laws thereof, escaping into another, shall, in consequence of any law or regulation therein, be discharged from such service or labor, but shall be delivered up on claim of the party to whom such service or labor may be due.]

This section
- Says that a citizen of one state who is in another state is entitled to all the rights and protection of the law of that state, just as if he or she were a resident there.
- Says that if a person commits a crime in one state and flees to another, the governor of the state where the crime was committed can demand that the accused be handed over, or extradited.
- [Refers to slaves escaping into another state and being returned. This portion was set aside by the 13th Amendment, which ended slavery.]

Section 3.

> New states may be admitted by the Congress into this union; but no new states shall be formed or erected within the jurisdiction of any other state; nor any state be formed by the junction of two or more states, or parts of states, without the consent of the legislatures of the states concerned as well as of the Congress.
>
> The Congress shall have power to dispose of and make all needful rules and regulations respecting the territory or other property belonging to the United States; and nothing in this Constitution shall be so construed as to prejudice any claims of the United States, or of any particular state.

This section
- Says that new states can't be made out of the territory of existing states without the permission of the state or states and the consent of Congress.
- Says that Congress is the highest legislative body for any U.S. territory that is not a state.

Section 4.

> The United States shall guarantee to every state in this union a republican form of government, and shall protect each of them against invasion; and on application of the legislature, or of the executive (when the legislature cannot be convened) against domestic violence.

This section
- Guarantees that the government will make sure that every state has a republican form of government — one in which people elect their representatives to Congress.
- Says that the federal government guarantees each state protection against invasion from foreign countries and can be called upon to protect a state from violent uprisings within the state.

Article V

This article sets out the rules for how the Constitution can be amended.

> The Congress, whenever two thirds of both houses shall deem it necessary, shall propose amendments to this Constitution, or, on the application of the legislatures of two thirds of the several states, shall call a convention for proposing amendments, which, in either case, shall be valid to all intents and purposes, as part of this Constitution, when ratified by the legislatures of three fourths of the several states, or by conventions in three fourths thereof, as the one or the other mode of

— continued on next page —

> *continued from previous page*
>
> ratification may be proposed by the Congress; [provided that no amendment which may be made prior to the year one thousand eight hundred and eight shall in any manner affect the first and fourth clauses in the ninth section of the first article; and that no state, without its consent, shall be deprived of its equal suffrage in the Senate.]

This article:

- Says that amendments may be proposed by a two-thirds vote of each part of Congress or by a national convention called by Congress at the request of two-thirds of the states. An amendment must then be ratified, or approved, by three-fourths of the states, either in their legislatures or at state conventions.

- [Guarantees the slavery provisions in Article I Section 9 cannot be amended before 1808.]

Article VI

This article makes the Constitution the supreme law of the United States.

> All debts contracted and engagements entered into, before the adoption of this Constitution, shall be as valid against the United States under this Constitution, as under the Confederation.
>
> This Constitution, and the laws of the United States which shall be made in pursuance thereof; and all treaties made, or which shall be made, under the authority of the United States, shall be the supreme law of the land; and the judges in every state shall be bound thereby, anything in the Constitution or laws of any State to the contrary notwithstanding.
>
> The senators and representatives before mentioned, and the members of the several state legislatures, and all executive and judicial officers, both of the United States and of the several states, shall be bound by oath or affirmation, to support this Constitution; but no religious test shall ever be required as a qualification to any office or public trust under the United States.

This article

- Promises that all debts and other bills owed by the United States government before the ratification of the Constitution will still be honored.

- Says that when state laws are in conflict with federal laws, the federal laws will be followed.

- Affirms that in order for a federal law to be valid, it must follow the Constitution.

- Says that federal and state officials must give their allegiance, or loyalty, to the U.S. Constitution above any state constitution or other law.
- Forbids the practice of favoring one religion over another in filling federal offices.

Article VII

This article ratified the Constitution.

> The ratification of the conventions of nine states, shall be sufficient for the establishment of this Constitution between the states so ratifying the same.
>
> Done in convention by the unanimous consent of the states present the seventeenth day of September in the year of our Lord one thousand seven hundred and eighty seven and of the independence of the United States of America the twelfth. In witness whereof we have hereunto subscribed our names,
>
> *George Washington — President and deputy from **Virginia***
>
>
>
> **New Hampshire**: *John Langdon, Nicholas Gilman*
> **Massachusetts**: *Nathaniel Gorham, Rufus King*
> **Connecticut**: *William Samuel Johnson, Roger Sherman*
> **New York**: *Alexander Hamilton*
> **New Jersey**: *William Livingston, David Brearly, William Paterson, Jonathan Dayton*
> **Pennsylvania**: *Benjamin Franklin, Thomas Mifflin, Robert Morris, George Clymer, Thomas FitzSimons, Jared Ingersoll, James Wilson, Gouverneur Morris*
> **Delaware**: *George Read, Gunning Bedford Jr., John Dickinson, Richard Bassett, Jacob Broom*
> **Maryland**: *James McHenry, Daniel of St Thomas Jenifer, Daniel Carroll*
> **Virginia**: *John Blair, James Madison, Jr.*
> **North Carolina**: *William Blount, Richard Dobbs Spaight, Hugh Williamson*
> **South Carolina**: *John Rutledge, Charles Cotesworth Pinckney, Charles Pinckney, Pierce Butler*
> **Georgia**: *William Few, Abraham Baldwin*

Faneuil Hall, Boston

The Amendments

NOTE TO TEACHER

Each of the 27 amendments to the Constitution has changed how the United States is governed. The first 10 amendments, the Bill of Rights, were created when it became clear that some states would not ratify the Constitution if the amendments were not added. Some of the following amendments extended the rights of citizens, including suffrage for African Americans, women, and people over the age of 18. Others clarify the rules for the presidency and members of Congress, and a few address social and political issues.

In this section, we look at what the amendments actually say and give a short breakdown of what they provide for. We suggest you copy these pages and hand them out to your class as reference for use later.

The Amendments

First Amendment — Freedom of Religion, Speech, and Press; the Rights to Assemble and Petition the Government

> Congress shall make no law respecting an establishment of religion, or prohibiting the free exercise thereof; or abridging the freedom of speech, or of the press; or the right of the people peaceably to assemble, and to petition the government for a redress of grievances.

The First Amendment guarantees five freedoms by prohibiting Congress from making laws that
- Establish a state religion or interfere with people practicing their religion.
- Interfere with freedom of speech.
- Interfere with freedom of the press.
- Prevent people from gathering.
- Prevent people from petitioning the government.

Second Amendment — The Right to Keep and Bear Arms

> A well-regulated militia, being necessary to the security of a free state, the right of the people to keep and bear arms, shall not be infringed.

There are two parts to this amendment:
- A "well-regulated militia" is necessary for the security of the nation.
- Accordingly, people have the right to keep and bear arms, or weapons.

Third Amendment — Limits on Housing Soldiers

> No soldier shall, in time of peace, be quartered in any house, without the consent of the owner, nor in time of war, but in a manner to be prescribed by law.

This amendment states that during peacetime, the military cannot force people to house or feed soldiers. However, Congress can make laws that require people to house and feed soldiers during times of war.

Fourth Amendment — Limiting Searches, Seizures, and Warrants

> The right of the people to be secure in their persons, houses, papers, and effects, against unreasonable searches and seizures, shall not be violated, and no warrants shall issue, but upon probable cause, supported by oath or affirmation, and particularly describing the place to be searched, and the persons or things to be seized.

There are three parts to this amendment:
- Citizens have the right to be secure from the government against "unreasonable searches and seizures."
- Warrants allowing the search of a citizen or his or her home can only be issued when there is probable cause to believe that a crime has been committed. A warrant has to be sworn to by an officer of the law in front of another officer of the law.
- In order for a search warrant to be valid, it must specifically describe the place to be searched and who or what is to be arrested or confiscated.

Fifth Amendment — Clarifying the Rights of the Accused

> No person shall be held to answer for a capital, or otherwise infamous crime, unless on a presentment or indictment of a grand jury, except in cases arising in the land or naval forces, or in the militia, when in actual service in time of war or public danger; nor shall any person be subject for the same offense to be twice put in jeopardy of life or limb; nor shall be compelled in any criminal case to be a witness against himself, nor be deprived of life, liberty, or property, without due process of law; nor shall private property be taken for public use, without just compensation.

There are five parts to this amendment:
- A person can only be put on trial for a serious crime after a grand jury decides that a good reason exists to put that person on trial. An exception exists for members of the armed forces, who, during war or a period of public danger, can be tried without a grand jury ruling.
- A person found not guilty by a court cannot be tried again for the same crime.
- Every person has the right to "due process of law" — the same legal process that everyone in society is entitled to. Due process includes rights found in, but not limited to, the Fifth, Sixth, Seventh, and Eighth Amendments.
- A person cannot be forced to testify, or speak in court, against her or himself.
- A person cannot have his or her property taken away for public use without being fairly paid for it. "Public use" includes land used for roads, land declared a national park, etc.

Sixth Amendment — Clarifying Rights in Criminal Cases

> In all criminal prosecutions, the accused shall enjoy the right to a speedy and public trial, by an impartial jury of the state and district wherein the crime shall have been committed, which district shall have been previously ascertained by law, and to be informed of the nature and cause of the accusation; to be confronted with the witnesses against him; to have compulsory process for obtaining witnesses in his favor, and to have the assistance of counsel for his defense.

This amendment protects many rights of the accused, including the right
- To a speedy public trial to be heard by a jury made up of people from the area where the crime took place.
- To be told what crimes he or she is standing trial for.
- To see and hear all witnesses who testify.
- To use witnesses for a defense.
- To have a lawyer.

Seventh Amendment — Clarifying Rights in Civil Cases

> In suits at common law, where the value in controversy shall exceed twenty dollars, the right of trial by jury shall be preserved, and no fact tried by a jury shall be otherwise reexamined in any court of the United States, than according to the rules of the common law.

This amendment has two parts:
- (Civil cases are non-criminal cases that usually involve people suing each other.) All common law, that is, civil, cases in a federal court that involve lawsuits between people for more than $20 must be tried by a jury. (In 1791, $20 was about 40 days worth of income for most people.)
- Individual cases cannot be retried in another federal court in the hope of winning a different result.

Eighth Amendment — Limiting Bails, Fines, and Punishments

> Excessive bail shall not be required, nor excessive fines imposed, nor cruel and unusual punishments inflicted.

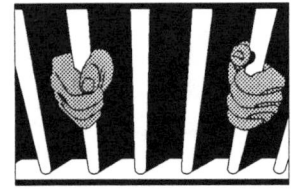

This amendment protects the individual by stating that
- Extremely high bail cannot be used to keep accused people in prison before their trials.
- Fines cannot be extremely high.
- Punishment cannot be "cruel and unusual."

Ninth Amendment — Clarifying the Rights of the People

> The enumeration in the Constitution, of certain rights, shall not be construed to deny or disparage others retained by the people.

This amendment states that the list of rights mentioned in the Constitution is not complete. Even though some rights may not be written down in the Constitution, the people still retain them.

Tenth Amendment — Clarifying States' Rights

> The powers not delegated to the United States by the Constitution, nor prohibited by it to the states, are reserved to the states respectively, or to the people.

This amendment assures the states that the powers not granted to the federal government in the Constitution are left to the states and to the people.

11th Amendment — Limiting Law Suits Against States

> The judicial power of the United States shall not be construed to extend to any suit in law or equity, commenced or prosecuted against one of the United States by citizens of another state, or by citizens or subjects of any foreign state.

This amendment is in direct response to a clause in Article III, Section 2, that extends judicial power to cases "between a state and citizens of another state." The 11th Amendment reverses that clause and makes it unconstitutional for a citizen of one state to sue another state in <u>federal</u> court.

12th Amendment — Electing the President and Vice President

> The electors shall meet in their respective states, and vote by ballot for President and Vice President, one of whom, at least, shall not be an inhabitant of the same state with themselves; they shall name in their ballots the person voted for as President, and in distinct ballots the person voted for as Vice President, and of the number of votes for each, which lists they shall sign and certify, and transmit, sealed, to the seat of government of the United States, directed to the president of the Senate; the president of the Senate shall, in the presence of the Senate and House of Representatives, open all the certificates and the

continued on next page

votes shall then be counted; the person having the greatest number of votes for President shall be the President, if such number be a majority of the whole number of electors appointed; and if no person have such majority, then from the person having the highest numbers not exceeding three on the list of those voted for as President, the House of Representatives shall choose immediately, by ballot, the President. But in choosing the President, the votes shall be taken by states, the representation from each state having one vote; a quorum for this purpose shall consist of a member or members from two-thirds of the states, and a majority of all the states shall be necessary to a choice. And if the House of Representatives shall not choose a President whenever the right of choice shall devolve upon them, before the fourth day of March next following, then the Vice President shall act as President, as in the case of the death or other constitutional disability of the President. The person having the greatest number of votes as Vice President, shall be the Vice President, if such number be a majority of the whole number of electors appointed, and if no person have a majority, then from the two highest numbers on the list, the Senate shall choose the Vice President; a quorum for the purpose shall consist of two-thirds of the whole number of Senators, and a majority of the whole number shall be necessary to a choice. But no person constitutionally ineligible to the office of President shall be eligible to that of Vice President of the United States.

The 12th Amendment provides that members of the Electoral College, called electors, vote for one person as president and another as vice president.

13th Amendment — Ending Slavery

SECTION 1. Neither slavery nor involuntary servitude, except as a punishment for crime whereof the party shall have been duly convicted, shall exist within the United States, or any place subject to their jurisdiction.

SECTION 2. Congress shall have power to enforce this article by appropriate legislation.

There are three parts to this amendment:
- Slavery shall not exist in the United States.
- The only involuntary servitude allowed is the punishment for crimes. In order to receive this punishment, a person has to have been convicted in a court.
- Congress has the right to pass laws to enforce this amendment.

14TH Amendment — Expanding the Rights and Protections of Citizens

SECTION 1. All persons born or naturalized in the United States and subject to the jurisdiction thereof, are citizens of the United States and of the state wherein they reside. No state shall make or enforce any law which shall abridge the privileges or immunities of citizens of the United States; nor shall any state deprive any person of life, liberty, or property, without due process of law; nor deny to any person within its jurisdiction the equal protection of the laws.

SECTION 2. Representatives shall be apportioned among the several states according to their respective numbers, counting the whole number of persons in each state, excluding Indians not taxed. But when the right to vote at any election for the choice of electors for President and Vice President of the United States, representatives of Congress, the executive and judicial officers of a state, or the members of the legislature thereof, is denied to any of the male inhabitants of such state, being twenty one years of age and citizens of the United States, or in any way abridged, except for participation in rebellion, or other crime, the basis of representation therein shall be reduced n the proportion which the number of such male citizens shall bear to the whole number of male citizens twenty one years of age in such state.

SECTION 3. No person shall be a senator or representative in Congress, or elector of President and Vice President, or hold any office, civil or military, under the United States, or under any state, who, having previously taken an oath, as a member of Congress, or as an officer of the United States, or as a member of any state legislature, or as an executive or judicial officer of any state, to support the Constitution of the United States, shall have engaged in insurrection or rebellion against the same, or given aid or comfort to the enemies thereof. But Congress may, by vote of two thirds of each house, remove such disability.

SECTION 4. The validity of the public debt of the United States, authorized by law, including debts incurred for payment of pensions and bounties for services in suppressing insurrection or rebellion, shall not be questioned. But neither the United States nor any state shall assume or pay any debt or obligation incurred in aid of insurrection or rebellion against the United States or any claim for the loss or emancipation of any slave; but all such debts, obligations, and claims shall be held illegal and void.

SECTION 5. The Congress shall have power to enforce, by appropriate legislation, the provisions of this article.

There are five distinct sections to this amendment:
- It asserts that all people born or naturalized in the United States are citizens of both the United States and of the state in which they live. No state can interfere with the rights of citizens and no state can deny anyone equal rights or equal protection under the law.
- It changes the way state populations are counted when determining congressional representation. Under this amendment, all people, except untaxed Indians, are counted in the census. This section then sets a punishment for any state that prevents a male citizen 21 years old or older from voting in a federal election by reducing that state's congressional representation.
- It prevents any former presidents, vice presidents, members of Congress or other officials who joined the Confederacy from returning to federal government jobs without the approval of two-thirds of the members of each house of Congress.
- It recognizes any debt incurred by the Union during the Civil War, but not those of the Confederacy. That is, Union debts are rightful debts and should be paid. Confederate debts are not recognized and don't have to be paid. The U.S. will not pay the South for the loss of any slaves.
- It states that Congress has the right to pass laws to enforce this amendment

15TH Amendment — Legalizing African American Suffrage

> SECTION 1. The right of citizens of the United States to vote shall not be denied or abridged by the United States or any state on account of race, color, or previous condition of servitude.
>
> SECTION 2. The Congress shall have power to enforce this article by appropriate legislation.

This amendment has two parts:
- No citizen shall be prevented from voting based on race or color or because that person once was a slave.
- Congress has the power to make laws to enforce this amendment.

16TH Amendment — Income Tax

> The Congress shall have the power to lay and collect taxes on incomes, from whatever source derived, without apportionment among the several states, and without regard to any census or enumeration.

This amendment is in direct response to the taxation rules defined in Article I, Section 9 of the Constitution. The 16th Amendment reverses a clause that prohibited direct taxes and makes it constitutional for the federal government to collect income tax from citizens no matter where they live in the United States.

17th Amendment — Electing Senators Directly

SECTION 1. The Senate of the United States shall be composed of two senators from each state, elected by the people thereof, for six years; and each senator shall have one vote. The electors in each state shall have the qualifications requisite for electors of the most numerous branch of the state legislatures.

SECTION 2. When vacancies happen in the representation of any state in the Senate, the executive authority of such state shall issue writs of election to fill such vacancies: provided that the legislature of any state may empower the executive thereof to make temporary appointments until the people fill the vacancies by election as the legislature may direct.

SECTION 3. This amendment shall not be so construed as to affect the election or term of any senator chosen before it becomes valid as part of the Constitution.

This amendment has three parts:
- United States senators must be directly elected by the people of their states.
- Any vacancies in the Senate must be filled by a special election of the people. In the interim, the state legislature may appoint someone to temporarily fill the office.
- The 17th Amendment did not affect any senators who were in office when it was ratified.

18th Amendment — Prohibition

After one year from the ratification of this article the manufacture, sale, or transportation of intoxicating liquors within, the importation thereof into, or the exportation thereof from, the United States and all territory subject to the jurisdiction thereof for beverage purpose is hereby prohibited.

SECTION 2. The Congress and the several states shall have concurrent power to enforce this article by appropriate legislation.

SECTION 3. This article shall be inoperative unless it shall have been ratified as an amendment to the Constitution by the legislatures of the several states, as provided in the Constitution, within seven years from the date of the submission hereof to the states by the Congress.

There are three parts to this amendment:
- One year after the amendment was ratified, it became illegal to make, sell, or transport alcoholic beverages in the United States, bring them into or ship them out of the country.

- Congress and the states share the power to make the laws to enforce this amendment.
- In order for this amendment to take effect, it had to be ratified by three-fourths of the state legislatures within seven years after Congress passed it with the necessary two-thirds support in each house.

19TH Amendment — Legalizing Woman Suffrage

SECTION 1. The right of citizens of the United States to vote shall not be denied or abridged by the United States or by any state on account of sex.

SECTION 2. Congress shall have the power to enforce this article by appropriate legislation.

This amendment has two parts:
- No citizen can be prevented from voting based on his or her sex.
- Congress has the power to make laws to enforce this amendment.

20TH Amendment — Clarifying Presidential and Congressional Terms

SECTION 1. The terms of the President and Vice President shall end at noon on the 20th day of January, and the terms of senators and representatives at noon on the 3rd day of January, of the years in which such terms would have ended if this article had not been ratified; and the terms of their successors shall then begin.

SECTION 2. The Congress shall assemble at least once in every year, and such meeting shall begin at noon on the 3rd day of January, unless they shall by law appoint a different day.

SECTION 3. If at the time fixed for the beginning of the term of the President, the President-elect shall have died, the Vice President-elect shall become President. If a President shall not have been chosen before the time fixed for the beginning of his term, or if the President-elect shall have failed to qualify, then the Vice President-elect shall act as President until a President shall have qualified; and the Congress may by law provide the case wherein neither a President-elect nor a Vice President-elect shall have qualified, declaring who shall then act as President, or the manner in which one who is to act shall be selected, and such person shall act accordingly until a President or Vice President shall have qualified.

continued on next page

---- *continued from previous page* ----

SECTION 4. The Congress may by law provide for the case of the death of any of the persons from whom the House of Representatives may choose a President whenever the right of choice shall have devolved upon them, and for the case of the death of any of the persons from whom the Senate may choose a Vice President whenever the right of choice shall have devolved upon them.

SECTION 5. Sections 1 and 2 shall take effect on the 15th day of October following the ratification of this article.

SECTION 6. This article shall be inoperative unless it shall have been ratified as an amendment to the Constitution by the legislatures of three fourths of the several states with seven years from the date of its submission.

This amendment has six sections:
- Terms for the president, vice president, and members of Congress have new starting and finishing dates. New sessions of Congress begin at noon on January 3rd, while the terms for president and vice president begin at noon on January 20th in the years in which the old terms are scheduled to end.
- Congress must meet at least one time each year, and that meeting will be at noon on January 3rd, unless a law selecting a different date is approved.
- If the person elected president dies before taking office, the vice president-elect becomes president. If a president isn't chosen before the beginning of the term, or if the president-elect is not qualified to serve, then the vice president-elect acts as president until a qualified president is chosen. If neither the president-elect nor the vice president-elect are qualified to serve, Congress shall select the president or establish rules to select one.
- If Congress is in the situation mentioned in the section above, choosing the president and vice president, and one or both of the candidates dies while under consideration, the House of Representatives may pass a law to determine how to choose a president and the Senate may pass a law to determine how to choose a vice president.
- The first two sections of this amendment took effect on October 15th after the amendment was ratified.
- The amendment was considered ratified only after three-fourths of the state legislatures approved it within seven years after Congress officially sent it to the states for approval.

21ST Amendment — Repealing Prohibition

> 1. The eighteenth article of amendment to the Constitution of the United States is hereby repealed.
>
> 2. The transportation or importation into any state, territory, or possession of the United States for delivery or use therein of intoxicating liquors, in violation of the laws thereof, is hereby prohibited.
>
> 3. This article shall be inoperative unless it shall have been ratified as an amendment to the Constitution by conventions in the several states, as provided in the Constitution, within seven years from the date of the submission hereof to the states by the Congress.

This amendment has three parts:
- The 18th Amendment is no longer valid.
- Any state or territory of the United States has the right to pass laws prohibiting the delivery or use of intoxicating liquors. If areas pass such laws, it is illegal to transport or import liquor into these areas.
- This amendment was ratified only after three-fourths of all state conventions approved it within seven years from the date Congress passed the amendment on to the states.

22ND Amendment — Limiting Presidents to Two Terms

> 1. No person shall be elected to the office of the President more than twice, and no person who has held the office of President, or acted as President, for more than two years of a term to which some other person was elected President shall be elected to the office of the President more than once. But this article shall not apply to any person holding the office of President when this article was proposed by the Congress, and shall not prevent any person who may be holding the office of President, or acting as President, during the term within which this article becomes operative from holding the office of President or acting as President during the remainder of such term.
>
> 2. This article shall be inoperative unless it shall have been ratified as an amendment to the Constitution by the legislatures of three-fourths of the several states within seven years from the date of its submission to the states by the Congress.

This amendment has two parts:
- No person can be elected president more than twice. If a president has served more than two years of another president's term, then he or she can only be elected one time instead of two. This amendment does not affect any president who is in office at the time of its ratification.

- The amendment had to be ratified by three-fourths of the state legislatures within seven years from the time Congress approved it and sent it to the states.

23RD Amendment — Legalizing Suffrage in Washington D.C. for Presidential Elections

1. The district constituting the seat of government of the United States shall appoint in such manner as the Congress may direct: A number of electors of President and Vice President equal to the whole number of senators and representatives in Congress to which the District would be entitled if it were a state, but in no event more than the least populous state; they shall be in addition to those appointed by the States, but they shall be considered, for the purposes of the election of President and Vice President, to be electors appointed by a state; and they shall meet in the district and perform such duties as provided by the twelfth article of amendment.

2. Congress shall have the power to enforce this article by appropriate legislation.

This amendment has two parts:
- It gives citizens in the District of Columbia the right to vote in presidential elections. The District is allotted the number of electors it would receive if it was a state. However, it can receive no more electors than the smallest state in the Union.
- Congress has the right to pass laws to carry out this amendment.

24TH Amendment — Ending the Poll Tax in Federal Elections

1. The right of citizens of the United States to vote in any primary or other election for President or Vice President, for electors for President or Vice President, or for senator or representative in Congress, shall not be denied or abridged by the United States or any state by reason of failure to pay any poll tax or other tax.

2. The Congress shall have power to enforce this article by appropriate legislation.

This amendment has two parts:
- It forbids the United States from requiring citizens to pay a poll tax or any other kind of tax in order to vote in federal elections.
- It gives Congress the power to pass laws to carry out this amendment.

25th Amendment: Clarifying Presidential Succession and Disability

SECTION 1. In case of the removal of the President from office or of his death or resignation, the Vice President shall become President.

SECTION 2. Whenever there is a vacancy in the office of the Vice President, the President shall nominate a Vice President who shall take the office upon confirmation by a majority vote of both houses of Congress.

SECTION 3. Whenever the President transmits to the president pro tempore of the Senate and the speaker of the House of Representatives his written declaration that he is unable to discharge the powers and duties of his office, and until he transmits to them a written declaration to the contrary, such powers and duties shall be discharged by the Vice President to the acting President.

SECTION 4. Whenever the Vice President and a majority of either the principal officers of the executive departments or of such other body as Congress may by law provide, transmit to the president pro tempore of the Senate and the Speaker of the House of Representatives their written declaration that the President is unable to discharge the powers and duties of his office, the Vice President shall immediately assume the powers and duties of the office as acting President.

Thereafter, when the President transmits to the president pro tempore of the Senate and the speaker of the House of Representatives his written declaration that no inability exists, he shall resume the powers and duties of his office unless the Vice President and a majority of either the principal officers of the executive departments or of such other body as Congress may by law provide, transmit within four days to the president pro tempore of the Senate and the speaker of the House of Representatives their written declaration that the President is unable to discharge the powers and duties of his office. Thereupon Congress shall decide the issue, assembling within 48 hours for that purpose if not in session. If the Congress, within 21 days after receipt of the latter written declaration, or if Congress is not in session, within 21 days after Congress is required to assemble, determines by two thirds vote of both houses that the President is unable to discharge the powers and duties of his office, the Vice President shall continue to discharge the same as active President; otherwise, the President shall assume the powers and duties of his office.

This amendment has four parts:
- If the president dies, resigns, or is removed from office, the vice president becomes president.

- If the office of the vice president is empty, the president shall choose a new vice president who can take office after being approved by the majority of both houses of Congress.
- If the president is aware that he or she will be unable to perform the duties of the presidency, he or she can write a letter to the leaders of the House and Senate and transfer all powers to the vice president. To reacquire the powers, he or she must write another letter to the leaders of Congress.
- If the vice president and at least half of the members of the president's cabinet believe that the president is unable to return to office after temporarily transferring his or her powers to the vice president, the vice president remains acting president until Congress decides who shall lead the country. If two-thirds of each house of Congress agree with the vice president's assessment of the president, then the president cannot return to office. If less than two-thirds of each house support the vice president, the president resumes the powers and duties of the presidency.

26TH Amendment — Suffrage for Citizens 18 Years of Age or Older

> SECTION 1. The right of citizens of the United States, who are 18 years of age or older, to vote shall not be denied or abridged by the United States or any state on account of age.
>
> SECTION 2. The Congress shall have the power to enforce this article by appropriate legislation.

This amendment has two parts:
- All citizens 18 years of age or older have the right to vote in federal and state elections.
- Congress can pass any laws necessary to enforce this amendment.

27TH Amendment — Limiting Congressional Pay

> No law, varying the compensation for the services of the senators and representatives, shall take effect, until an election of representatives shall have intervened.

This amendment states that a congressional election must take place before pay raises for members of Congress can take effect.

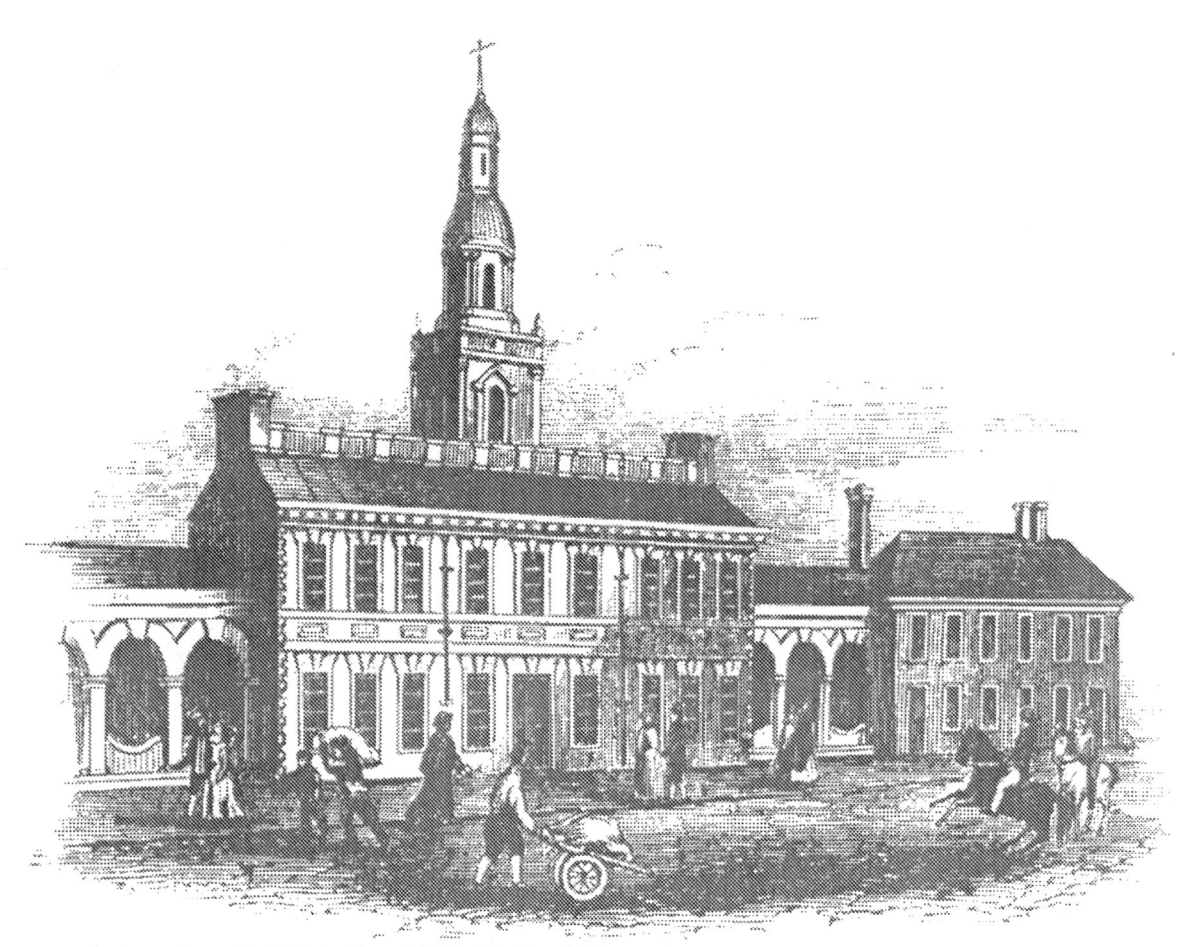
Independence Hall (State House), Philadelphia, 1774

Activities for the Articles

NOTE TO TEACHER

These activities will help your students better understand what each of the articles of the Constitution means. We suggest that students have a copy of the portion of the articles you want to cover. The annotated articles are printed elsewhere in this resource book.

The activities for the articles include discussion questions, research/discussion questions, role plays, and essay questions. We encourage you to adapt any or all of these elements for your own use. For example, in many cases essay questions can also be used as class discussion questions, and vice versa.

Activities for the Articles

Preamble

Research/Discussion

The preamble to the Constitution has five phrases that define the objectives of the United States:

> establish justice
>
> insure domestic tranquillity
>
> provide for the common defense
>
> promote the general welfare
>
> secure the blessings of liberty to ourselves and our posterity

Divide the class into five groups and have the members of each group examine one of these phrases. What does the phrase mean literally? What was it referring to in 1787, when the writers of the Constitution included it? What does it mean today?

Each group should present its findings to the class. After the presentations, discuss the following questions:

- When the framers wrote "We the people" in the Preamble they were stating that the people of the United States — not the states themselves — were creating the Constitution and setting up the system of government. By doing this, the framers signaled that the people as a whole were more powerful than the states. Why do you think they wanted to make that clear?

- Do you think the phrases in the Preamble are a good way to start a document that sets down the rules for how a country is to be run? Why or why not?

The Preamble calls for "a more perfect union." Many experts say these words mean the framers wanted the Constitution to set up better rules for running the country than the Articles of Confederation did.

The Articles of Confederation were passed in 1781 and lasted less than eight years, until the Constitution went into effect on July 17, 1788. George Washington, James Madison, Benjamin Franklin, and others called a convention to draft a new Constitution because they saw weaknesses in the Articles of Confederation.

The Articles of Confederation made the following provisions, among others:
- It guaranteed that the states were independent of each other and the national government.

- It said the states were connected into a "firm league of friendship."
- It required each state to keep an army.
- It provided for just one branch of central, national government, which it called "Congress."
- It gave Congress the power, with a majority vote, to declare war and make peace with foreign countries, make treaties with foreign countries, settle boundary disputes between states, make new states, regulate and borrow money, and set up a postal system. Congress could also appoint one of its members to be president. The president's job was to run Congress's meetings.
- It required that any changes in the Articles had to be passed by the legislatures of every state.

There was no executive or judicial branch under the Articles of Confederation.

Divide the class into five groups. The members of each group should do research on one of the following questions:
- Why didn't the newly formed states want an executive or judicial branch in the national government?
- There is nothing in the Articles of Confederation about trade between states. How was trade handled? What happened when there were disputes?
- What problems happened because there was no national army?
- What led the framers of the Constitution to call for a constitutional convention? Why did they think the Articles of Confederation weren't working?
- Who were the Federalists and who were the Anti-Federalists? Who were some of their leaders and what arguments did they make for what they believed in?

Have members of each group present their group's findings to the class. Then discuss the following questions:
- Do you think a government can be effective if it doesn't have an executive and a judicial branch?
- Do you think it can be effective without a national army?
- Do you think it's better for the states as a whole to be stronger than the federal government? Why or why not?
- What do you think the United States would be like today under the Articles of Confederation?

Essay

- What was Shays's Rebellion? Why did it help lead to the Constitutional Convention?

- Research and write a short essay about one of the trade disputes among the states under the Articles of Confederation. What was the dispute about? What happened during the dispute? How was the dispute resolved?

- What were the main arguments of the Federalists for a strong national government? What were the main arguments of the Anti-Federalists for a weak national government — or no national government at all? Which side do you agree with more? Why?

- Why did the governing bodies of the 13 new states want the Articles of Confederation to be the rules for their new national government in 1781? What happened in the United States at this time to cause the supporters of the Articles of Confederation to feel this way?

Article I

Section 1.

Discussion

Having two parts of Congress may seem normal today, but it was unusual when the framers sat down to hammer out the Constitution. The two-house Congress was one of the most important compromises, or agreements, of the Constitutional Convention. The convention almost fell apart before this "Great Compromise" was reached. At first, the small states wanted the "New Jersey plan," which called for each state to have the same number of representatives. The bigger states argued for the "Virginia plan," which called for representation based on population — the more people there were in a state, the more representatives the state would have. With this in mind, discuss the following questions:

- Why do you think the small states favored the New Jersey plan and the large states wanted the Virginia plan?

- From what you know today, how did the members of the Constitutional Convention reach the "Great Compromise" between the New Jersey and Virginia plans?

- Do you think the compromise worked? That is, do you think having two parts of Congress is good for the United States? Why or why not?

Essay

- Who in the New Jersey delegation proposed the New Jersey plan? Who proposed the Virginia plan? Who came up with the "Great Compromise"? How did these people come up with the compromise that led to the two parts of Congress?

Section 2.

Discussion

This section establishes how the House of Representatives is run. Discuss the following questions with the class:

- There are 435 members of the House of Representative. How many representatives does your state have? Who is your representative in Congress? Do you know the names of any other representatives from your state?

- The number of representatives each state has is based on population. That's why a census is called for in this part of Article I. What happens if a state loses population and another state gains it?

- The qualifications required of members of the House of Representatives are lower than those required for any other elected office in the federal government. Do you think this is good or bad? Why do you think the writers of the Constitution said a representative only had to be 25 years old and a citizen of the nation for just seven years?

- Why do you think the framers limited the terms of House members to two years? Do you think this is too short a time? Why or why not?

- The Constitution leaves it up to the states to decide who can and can't vote for members of the House. Why do you think the writers of the Constitution did this?

- Every ten years, the U.S. takes a census, as is called for in this section. The census doesn't simply count people. It counts them by sex, race, age, how much they earn each year, and so on. Some people think the census should be taken by "sampling." These people think census takers can find out all this information by taking a scientific sample of people living in an area. Those who support sampling say this method of conducting the census will save millions of dollars. Those who oppose sampling say the only true way to find out how many people live in the United States is to count them all. Which side do you agree with more? Why?

- The House is responsible for bringing impeachment charges, or accusations of crimes, against high public officials. Why do you think the framers of the Constitution gave the House this power?

Short essay

- The national census is taken every ten years. From what you read in the Constitution and elsewhere, how does the census affect how people are represented in the House of Representatives? Over the years, which states have lost the most representatives and which states have gained the most?

- In 1929, Congress limited the number of people in the House of Representatives to 435. How could Congress do this without actually changing the Constitution? Why did Congress set the number of representatives at 435? How many representatives would there be today if there was one for every 30,000 people, as was originally called for in Article I Section 2?

Essay

- Most of Section 2 has either been changed since it was written or has become outdated. For example, "three-fifths of all other people" tells how slaves were counted in national censuses. Research this part of Section 2 and find out why slaves were counted in this way. What conflict between slave states and non-slave states led to this phrase? Why did the slave states think it was important? Why did non-slave states go along with the wording? Did this part of Section 2 have anything to do with the Civil War? Explain your findings in an essay.

Section 3.

Discussion

This section establishes how the Senate is run. Discuss the following questions with the class:

- The first part of Section 3 was changed by the 17th Amendment. Why do you think the framers of the Constitution originally wanted senators to be appointed by state legislatures and not directly elected by the citizens?

- Senators serve six-year terms. Every two years, one-third of them are up for election. Why do you think the Constitution calls for this? Why do you think all senators aren't elected every six years, in the same way that all representatives are elected every two years?

- The House of Representatives brings impeachment charges against public officials, and the Senate tries them. In order to bring charges against a high official, the House only has to have the approval of a simple majority — that is, more than half of its members. In order to convict someone on impeachment charges, the Senate needs a two-thirds vote. Why do you think the system is set up this way? Why is it harder to convict someone than to charge that person?

Section 4.

Essay

- When the Constitution was written, the framers thought it was very important to have Congress meet at least once a year. This is something we take for granted now — Congress is usually in session for most of the year. The framers' concerns about how often Congress should meet go back to practices in England in the centuries leading up to the writing of the U.S. Constitution. What were the events and practices in England that led to these concerns? Why did the framers think it was important to have Congress meet at least once a year? Why did they feel it was so important to spell this requirement out? What does this tell you about the times the framers were living in?

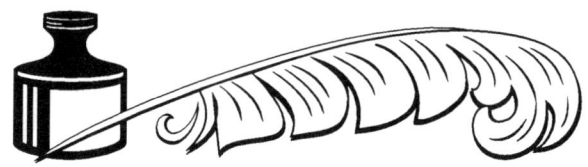

Section 5.

Role play

Each part of Congress is responsible for policing the actions of its members. If someone violates the procedures of either part of Congress or commits some sort of crime, that person can be punished. The usual forms of punishment are censure, reprimand, and expulsion. Censure is the formal condemnation of a member's actions, read aloud while the accused stands before the entire body of legislators. The House sometimes uses a reprimand, which is similar to censure except it doesn't require the member to be present when the condemnation is read. When a member is expelled, he or she is thrown out of office.

In this role play, have the class act as Congress and judge the following situations. The class is to decide by voting whether each member of Congress should be censured, reprimanded, expelled, or acquitted (that is, found not guilty of the charges). The examples are all based on actual cases. In brackets following each example, you'll find the actual outcome of the case. You may want to share these outcomes with the students after they vote.

Assault on a senator — During a heated debate over slavery in 1856, a member of the House of Representatives walked over to the U.S. Senate and beat a senator with a cane after the senator had made insulting remarks about the attacker's uncle. The attacker fled to his home in South Carolina, where he died a year later. The attacker was assisted by another member of the House who prevented members of the Senate from stopping the attack. Should the man who helped the attacker be censured, reprimanded, expelled, or acquitted? [Rep. Laurence M. Keit was censured for assisting Rep. Preston S. Brooks in his attack on Sen. Charles Sumner.]

An investigating senator — A controversial senator conducted investigations of government agencies because he said they were run by communists. His Senate investigations were closely watched by the general public. The senator never found any communists and was investigated himself. A Senate committee investigated his finances, and he was accused of being abusive to the committee members. Should the senator be censured, reprimanded, expelled, or acquitted? [Senator Joseph McCarthy was censured in 1954.]

A representative accused of taking a bribe — Members of the FBI posed as rich Arabs from the Middle East who wanted to influence Congress members. The FBI team bribed one senator and six representatives, who were all put on trial and convicted. All but one of the representatives resigned their offices or were voted out before being convicted of taking bribes at their trials. What should happen to the remaining representative? Should he be censured, reprimanded, expelled, or acquitted? [Rep. Michael J. Myers was expelled.]

Short essay

A tradition in the Senate, filibusters are long debates or speeches designed to delay voting on a bill. Do research to answer one of the following questions about filibusters. You may want to discuss your findings as a class.

- When were filibusters used the most? What bills were they used to delay or stop? Who delivered the longest filibuster and what was that filibuster against?

- What is the procedure for stopping filibusters?

- Why doesn't the House have any trouble with filibusters?

Section 6.

Discussion

This section talks about congressional immunity. Generally speaking, a member of Congress can say anything — including lies and slander — on the floor of the House or Senate and not be taken to court over it. With the class, discuss the following questions:

- Why do you think the framers of the Constitution included congressional immunity in this article?

- Do you think it's right or wrong that members of Congress enjoy immunity on the floors of the House and Senate? Why?

Section 7.

Research/Discussion

This section outlines the complicated procedure for passing a bill into law. It is part of the separation of powers that the framers of the Constitution felt was crucial to the system of government they set up for the United States. Assign members of the class to research and report on the following questions:

- What does "separation of powers" mean? How is the separation of powers presented in Article I Section 7 of the Constitution?

- What is a veto? What is a pocket veto? How do these measures relate to the separation of powers?

- Why do both parts of Congress have to pass a bill before it goes to the president for signing?

- Why was the House of Representatives given the power to start all money and taxation bills? (This is the most important power of the House.)

- Why do you think a presidential veto must be overturned by a two-thirds vote of both parts of Congress?

After the presentation of the reports, have the class discuss the following:

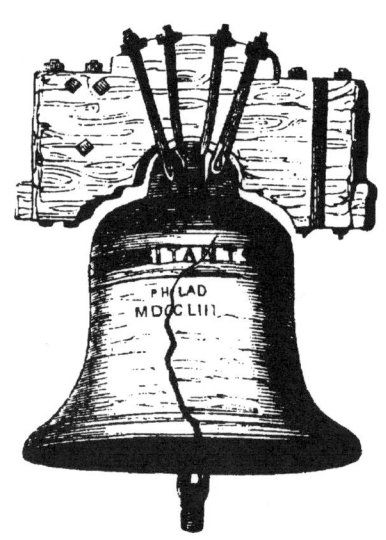

- Do you think the way bills must be passed in order to become law is too complicated? Why or why not? If so, how would you change the process?

- Do you think it's right or wrong that the president has the power to veto a bill that Congress passes? Why?

- Why do you think the framers of the Constitution thought separation of powers was so important? Do you think it's important? Why or why not? If you don't think this system is important, what, if anything, would you replace it with?

Section 8.

Research/Discussion

This section details the powers Congress has. Have small groups or individual members of the class research and figure out what the following powers mean:

> To borrow money on the credit of the United States.
>
> To regulate commerce with foreign nations, and among the several states, and with the Indian tribes.
>
> To promote the progress of science and art.
>
> To declare war . . . and make rules concerning capture on land and water.
>
> To raise and support armies [and] to provide and maintain a navy.
>
> To provide for calling forth the militia to execute the laws of the union, suppress insurrections and repel invasions.
>
> To make all laws which shall be necessary and proper for carrying into execution the foregoing powers.

After the class members or groups give their reports, discuss the following with the class as a whole:

- The "commerce clause" in this section — that is, the clause that allows Congress to regulate commerce with foreign countries and Indian tribes, and among the states — was passed without any sort of debate at the Constitutional Convention. From what you've learned about the Articles of Confederation, why do you suppose this clause was approved by everyone at the convention? To answer this question, you may want to do some research on the history of this clause and on the Articles of Confederation.

- Why do you think Congress was given the power not only to "lay and collect taxes," but also to borrow money?

- How does Congress promote the progress of science and art? How did Congress promote these things at the time the Constitution was written?

- The last clause in this section has often been called the "elastic clause," the "implied powers" clause, or the "necessary and proper clause." Why do you think this clause is called all those names? What do you think it gives Congress the power to do?

Essay

- Most of this section enumerates the powers Congress has — that is, it specifically states what Congress can do. The last clause *implies* that Congress can do much more. It gives Congress the power to pass any law "necessary and proper" to carry out its other powers. Take a look at this section of the Articles and at the powers that are spelled out and find three cases in which you think Congress was also given implied powers. In other words, in what situations do you think Congress would need to take more powers than are specifically mentioned in Article I Section 8 in order to carry out its duties? An example would be the clause that gives Congress the power to establish post offices. That clause also *implies* that Congress has the power to have stamps issued or to make laws against mail fraud. Explain your findings and discuss the additional implied powers that you think this section grants to Congress.

- The Supreme Court case *McCullough v. Maryland* was very important in giving Congress a lot of power. Research and give a written report on what this case was about and how it increased the power of Congress.

Section 9.

Research/Discussion

There are eight powers denied to Congress in this section. Assign eight class members or small groups to examine and do research on these powers. Make sure the students find out and explain what all the words and phrases in this section mean. Why did the framers deny these powers to Congress?

Have the class members or groups deliver their reports to the class and then discuss the following questions:

- Why do you think Congress could not ban the importation of slaves before 1808? What happened after 1808?

- Why do you think the framers didn't allow the passage of ex post facto laws and bills of attainder?

- Why do you think the framers of the Constitution were so opposed to granting titles of nobility?

- Why do you think Congress was forbidden to suspend the writ of habeas corpus?

- Today, many states get federal funds because they have military bases. Other states get very little or no federal money because they don't have military bases. Favoring one state over another through regulating commerce or revenue is forbidden in this section. Do you think granting federal monies to states with military bases violates this section of the Articles? Why or why not?

Section 10.

Research/Discussion

Have individual students or groups research and put into their own words the three parts of this section. After they give their reports to the class, discuss the following questions:

- Why do you suppose states can't make treaties with other countries?

- Why do you think the framers of the Constitution felt it was important to limit the power of both Congress and the states? Why do you suppose they didn't do the same for the executive branch?

- What parts of this section do you think were used by the North as a reason for not allowing the South to secede from the Union before the Civil War?

Article II

Section 1.

Essay

The following research questions can be used as essay assignments or as a springboard for class discussion.

- The first three words of this section — "The executive power" — have been interpreted by many presidents as giving them "implied powers" — that is, powers not enumerated, or specifically stated, in the Constitution. Compare these words with the "necessary and proper" clause in Article I, Section 8, and the "judicial review" clause in Article III, Section 2. These two clauses are seen as giving more power to the legislative and judicial branches. What similarities or differences do you see among these three sets of words? Do you agree or disagree that the words "the executive power" give the president additional implied powers? Why?

- Presidents have often acted without the consent of Congress, especially in times of national crisis. The earliest example of a president who seemed to overstep his power was when President Jefferson authorized the Louisiana Purchase. What was the Louisiana Purchase? How did the president take on power to make the purchase? Was the purchase opposed? What did the president himself think of his action? Do you think it was a good or bad idea that the president went beyond his enumerated powers in this case? Why?

- The process of choosing the president was changed after the 1804 election. Up to that time, the president and vice president did not have to be from the same political party, or on the same "ticket" (that is, running together), in order to be elected to office. The 12th Amendment now seems to make sure that the president and vice president must be elected together. Do research on what happened during the 1804 election. Why do you think that election led to the 12th Amendment? Do you think the change was good or bad? Why?

- The framers of the Constitution created the electoral college because they were worried that the citizens of the United States were not informed or smart enough to choose a president and vice president themselves. Once in history, when Benjamin Harrison ran against Grover Cleveland, a candidate who won the popular vote (that is, he got the most votes in the general election) lost the electoral vote and, as a result, lost the presidency. In 1824, a candidate who received more electoral votes than any other candidate was denied the presidency. Research these two political campaigns. What happened in them? Why were the men who seemed to win denied office? Do you think the Electoral College is a good or bad way of choosing the president? Why? Do you think the Electoral College is still needed today? Why or why not?

- At what times in American history has a vice president succeeded a president during the president's term of office? What problems did these people have? How many of them were elected in their own right after serving out the term of a president who died or left office?

Section 2.

Essay

The following research questions can be used as essay assignments or as a springboard for class discussion.

- The president is commander-in-chief of the military, but only Congress can declare war. However, Congress did not declare war when the U.S. sent troops to Korea or to Vietnam. Pick one of these wars. How was the U.S. able to fight in this war without the approval of Congress? What did the president do to get the U.S. involved in this war without the consent of Congress? Do you think the president was right to use his power in this way, or should Congress have declared war before troops were sent into battle? Explain your answers.

- In 1973, Congress passed the War Powers Act. What is this act, and how does it affect how and under what conditions the U.S. can go to war? Has it been used since it was passed?

- Throughout history, the president has called out state militias and state National Guard units to restore order in various areas. Find one example of an occasion when the president did this. Why did he call out the guard? What happened after he did so?

- The president can pardon people for offenses, even if these people haven't been formally charged with anything. Two famous examples of this kind of presidential pardon are Gerald Ford's 1974 pardon of Richard Nixon, and George Bush's 1992 pardon of Caspar Weinberger. Pick one of these events, and write an essay about what happened and why the person was pardoned. What happened after the pardon?

- The president appoints many people to positions — that is, the president names individuals to fill jobs. Most of these appointments are made with the "advice and consent" of Congress. Usually, Senate or House committees hold hearings to interview the person who is being considered for an appointment. Then the committee recommends to Congress as a whole whether the appointment should be approved. In 1997, the president wanted to appoint the governor of Massachusetts to be ambassador to Mexico. A powerful senator disagreed with the appointment, and he refused even to hold hearings on whether or not the governor should get the job. As a result, the appointment didn't go through. Find out about this incident. Why did the senator oppose the appointment? Do you think it was right or wrong for the senator to refuse a hearing for the former governor? Why?

- The Constitution says the president is in charge of "making treaties" with the approval of Congress. Most presidents have taken this to mean that foreign policy — the official relations of the United States with other countries — is one of the responsibilities of the executive branch. Find two examples of times when a president's foreign policy was opposed by Congress. What happened to cause the disagreement between Congress and the president? How was the disagreement resolved?

Section 3.

Research/Discussion

Every year, the president delivers a State of the Union address before Congress. Many times, the president has used the State of the Union message to push for his own programs. Assign members of the class to research how presidents have pushed for their own ideas on each of the following national issues in their State of the Union addresses:

illegal drug use

the budget

welfare

smoking by young people

national defense

taxes

education

civil rights

Have the students present their findings to the class and then discuss the following questions as a group:

- Why do you think the Constitution calls for the president to give a State of the Union address?

- Do you think it's right or wrong for the president to advance his or her own ideas in this address? Why?

- Do you think the State of the Union address is important to how our country is run? Why or why not?

Section 4.

Research/Discussion

This section gives Congress the power to impeach high government officials, including the president and vice president, and remove them from office. Impeaching an official means charging an official with wrongdoing. Only one president — Andrew Johnson — has ever been impeached. However, historians agree that if he had not resigned, Richard Nixon would also have been impeached. The events that led to Mr. Nixon's resignation are known as "Watergate."

Divide the class into six groups and have each group do research on one of the following issues:

- What is the Watergate? What happened at the Watergate in June of 1972 that began the chain of events that brought down Mr. Nixon's presidency? Who were the major people involved, and what happened to them?

- Which part of Congress investigated the Watergate affair? What happened during the hearings this body held?

- What were the "Watergate tapes"? What importance did they have in the investigation? Who in the White House was involved in the Watergate matter?

- What was the Supreme Court's role in the Watergate affair? What were the events that led up to the Court's ruling on the matter? What did it decide?

- Why did Mr. Nixon resign? How close to impeachment was he when he decided to leave office? What happened after he resigned?

- How has the Watergate affair changed our government? How has it changed our society and how we view the executive branch? How has it changed how the Constitution has been interpreted?

After the groups present their reports to the class, discuss the following questions:

- Do you think Mr. Nixon should have resigned? Why or why not?

- If he had not resigned, do you think Mr. Nixon would have been impeached? Why or why not? Do you think he would have been convicted of wrongdoing by the Senate? Why or why not?

- Do you think the Watergate matter was serious enough to bring impeachment charges? Why or why not?

- What effect do you think the Watergate affair has had on the public's confidence in the press? In our public officials? In the Constitution's ability to deal with suspected wrongdoing in the government?

Article III

Before this article, there was no way to bring most questions of federal law into a federal court. Setting up a third branch of government — the judicial branch — was something new in the world when the Constitution was written.

Section 1.

Discussion

Section 1 talks about the Supreme Court. This section puts in place the final piece of the separation of powers outlined in the Constitution.

Before going on to the research/discussion activities, talk about this section of the Constitution with the class. Have the class read the section, or read it aloud to your students, before discussing these questions:

- From what you see here, what are the qualifications a Supreme Court justice must have? Are the qualifications for the chief justice — the leader of the Supreme Court — different from the qualifications for an associate justice?

- How many Supreme Court justices does the Constitution call for?

- How do justices get their jobs? Why do you think the framers of the Constitution said that the only way judges could be forced to leave office was to be impeached and convicted?

Research/Discussion

There have been more than 100 members of the Supreme Court. Have individual class members or small groups do research on the following justices and answer the questions listed below. (This activity can also be used as an essay assignment.)

John Marshall

Roger Taney

John Marshall Harlan I

Oliver Wendell Holmes

William Taft

Hugo Black

Felix Frankfurter

Louis Brandeis

Robert Jackson

Earl Warren

Thurgood Marshall

William Brennan

Harry Blackmun

Sandra Day O'Connor

When did the justice serve? Is this justice still serving? What did the person do before he or she was appointed to the court? Did the justice have trouble getting appointed to the court? What effect did the justice have on the Constitution? What effect did the justice have on our laws? What effect did the justice have on the court? What were some of the important cases the justice worked on? What is the justice known for on the court (that is, is he or she known to be liberal? conservative? moderate? Give examples. What are his or her most famous opinions?)

After the class members or groups have given their presentations, discuss the relative importance of these justices.

Essay

These research questions can be used as essay assignments or as a springboard for class discussion.

- How does the method by which Supreme Court justices and other federal judges are appointed and confirmed affect the separation of powers?

- The president appoints, or recommends, justices for the Supreme Court and judges for all the federal courts. But Congress must approve these justices and judges. Before it confirms a new justice or judge, Congress holds a hearing to determine whether the person is suited to the job. Often, these hearings are controversial. The most famous recent hearing about a Supreme Court justice involved Clarence Thomas. Research what happened when Mr. Thomas was appointed to the Supreme Court by then-President Bush. Where was his appointment hearing held? What happened during the hearing? What was the outcome? Do you agree with the decision? Do you think the hearing process was fair or unfair to Clarence Thomas? Why?

- The Supreme Court has varied in size from the beginning. Research some of the reasons the number of justices has changed. What happened in 1937 when President Roosevelt tried to "pack" the Supreme Court? What was his plan, and why did he want Congress to approve it?

Section 2.

Research/Role play

Have the class research what goes on when the Supreme Court hears a case. The class should learn the procedures involved and what happens during a Supreme Court session. Then set up a constitutional case to be heard by nine Supreme Court justices picked from the class. You may also want to pick a chief justice or act as the chief justice yourself. The case you pick can either be historical or something made up by you or the class. There should be one or more attorneys representing each side. The attorneys should research their arguments carefully and make sure to bring in the constitutional basis for their arguments. The justices should also research both sides of the case carefully, so they can ask the attorneys good questions.

The attorneys should prepare a written brief to give to the court and also prepare an oral argument to present before the court. Usually only one attorney from each side makes the actual oral arguments before the court. Each side has a limited amount of time to present its oral argument (have your students research how long an oral argument is allowed to run), and Supreme Court justices may interrupt the attorneys to question them during the presentation. Other interested groups may file "friend of the court," or "amicus," briefs, which support one side or the other.

After both sides present their cases, the justices should meet together and vote. The justices should decide the case based on their interpretation of the Constitution and on the arguments presented by the two sides and the "friends of the court." Remember, all nine justices don't have to agree. Whichever side gets a majority vote wins. The justices should then write their decisions, or "opinions." The majority opinion should be written by one justice who agrees with the decision that was made, with input from the other agreeing justices. The chief justice decides who will write the majority opinion. The other agreeing justices may wish to write concurring opinions, which support the decision that was made but do so for different reasons than the official majority opinion. Justices who disagree with the majority opinion should write dissenting opinions giving the reasons they disagree with the majority opinion. Have the justices present their findings in front of the class, and ask them to answer questions about how and why they formed their opinions.

After this activity, discuss the following questions:
- Do you think enough time is given to oral arguments before the Supreme Court? Why or why not? Do you think it's fair that Supreme Court justices can interrupt a presentation to ask questions? Why or why not?

- From your research and this activity, how important do you think concurring and dissenting opinions are? Why?

- What role, if any, do you think personal opinions play in how Supreme Court justices reach their decisions?

- Do you think cases that are decided by a Supreme Court vote of 9-0 have more "weight" than those decided by a 5-4 margin? Why or why not?

Essay

These research questions can be used as essay assignments or as a springboard for class discussion.

- This section of the Constitution is the basis for "judicial review," the important idea that the Supreme Court has the right to review laws that are brought before it and decide if they are constitutional. To learn more about judicial review, do research on the case of *Marbury v. Madison.* What happened in this case? How did the idea of judicial review grow out of this case?

- Has there ever been a time when a dissenting opinion has had an impact on later Supreme Court decisions? If so, when?

- One ongoing debate among legal experts — and members of the Supreme Court themselves — has to do with interpreting the Constitution. Some legal experts support a strict interpretation of the Constitution, while others support a broad interpretation. "Strict constructionists" believe that no meaning outside the words actually found in the Constitution should be applied to cases brought before the Supreme Court. "Broad constructionists" believe that many times, the words in the Constitution are too general to provide all the answers when deciding cases. Those who say the Constitution should be interpreted broadly say that words like "unreasonable search and seizure" and "cruel and unusual punishment" are vague and have to be interpreted. Strict constructionists think the Supreme Court has often gone too far in its interpretation of the Constitution. Do research on these two schools of thought. Pick a case in which you think the Constitution was broadly interpreted and one in which it was strictly interpreted. How do the cases compare? Do you think the justices reached the correct decisions in the cases? Do you agree with one decision more than the other? Do you think the Constitution should be interpreted loosely or strictly? Why?

- All courts, including the Supreme Court, rely on precedent in their rulings. What does it mean to say something is a legal precedent? Why does the Supreme Court rely on precedent? Why do the lower courts rely on it? How has legal precedent shaped the laws of our nation? Use any examples of court cases determined by legal precedent you can find to answer these questions.

- Are Supreme Court justices free from politics? Some experts say that the court's decisions usually follow the mood or political ideas that seem to be held by most people in the country. Do you agree or disagree? Why? Back up your opinion by referring to specific decisions the court has made.

Section 3.

Essay

- This section deals with treason, which the Constitution describes as American citizens "levying war" against the United States or "giving aid and comfort" to the country's enemies. Occasionally, trials for treason have been heard in federal courts and in the Supreme Court. Research either Aaron Burr or Julius and Ethel Rosenberg, the people at the center of the two most famous American treason cases. What happened in the case you chose? What was America like when the treason charges were made? How did the public react to the case? What did the lower courts and the Supreme Court find in the cases? Do you agree or disagree with these findings? Why? What happened to the people involved?

Article IV

Research/Discussion

This article was lifted from the Articles of Confederation and placed, almost word for word, into the Constitution. Ask students why they think this article was put into the Constitution. Why was it placed fourth in the list of articles? Why did the framers of the Constitution think it was important to use this part of the Articles of Confederation in the Constitution?

Section 1.

Research/Discussion

This section says that states must uphold the laws of other states. Have members of the class do research on this issue, then discuss the following questions with the class as a whole:

- Do all states recognize each others' marriage laws?

- Do all states recognize each others' divorce laws?

- Suppose a young person in one state can leave school at the age of 16 and does so. The youth travels to another state, where the minimum age for leaving school is set at 18. Does he or she have to go back to school?

Section 2.

Research/Discussion

These research questions can be used as essay assignments or as a springboard for class discussion.

This part of the Constitution contains a section that helped lead to the Civil War. The section says that a slaveholder can go anywhere — even into nonslave states or territories — to chase and capture escaped slaves. This section was later overturnd by the 13th Amendment. However, this part of the Constitution did not stop some citizens in the North from helping slaves escape. Divide the class into five groups and have each group research one of the following questions:

- What was the Fugitive Slave Law? How did people in the North react to this law?

- What was the Underground Railroad? What routes did this railroad take? Who did the railroad serve? Who were some of the people who ran this railroad? Where were some of the stops along the railroad? How effective was it?

- Research how the book *Uncle Tom's Cabin* brought attention to slavery and fugitive slaves. How did this book affect public opinion in the years leading up to the Civil War?

- Who were the abolitionists? What did they do to fight slavery? Name some of the most famous abolitionists and briefly describe what these people did.

- What was your state's (or territory's) position on the question of slavery? What was your state's position in the Civil War? How did your state government deal with the slavery issue in the years leading up to the Civil War and during the war itself?

Have members of the groups present their findings to the entire class and answer questions about their research.

This section also says that people who are citizens of one state have the same rights as citizens in other states when they travel to those states. It goes on to say that people can't run away to another state in order to avoid paying for a crime. When one state delivers a criminal who has run away back to the state he or she ran from, it is called "extradition."

Have members of the class research the following questions and present their findings to the class:

- What is extradition? What process is used when one state extradites someone from another state? When might extradition not be used?

- How long does your state require people to be residents before they can vote? Before they can collect welfare?

After the presentations, discuss the following questions:

- Do you think it's fair or right that one state can extradite fugitives to another state?

- Why do you think the framers of the Constitution included this section in the articles?

Section 3.

Short essay

This part of Article IV has to do with the formation of new states. Students can answer the following research questions in short essays or discuss the questions as a class:

- When was your state admitted to the United States? What steps did it go through to become a state?

- What was the last state to enter the U.S.? When did it happen? How did it happen?

- The state of West Virginia is unusual in that it was made from another state — a procedure that seems to go against the Constitution. How did West Virginia become a state?

- Recently, some lawmakers have proposed making Puerto Rico the 51st state in the U.S. The citizens of Puerto Rico are unsure whether they want Puerto Rico to become a state. What is Puerto Rico's status now? How did it gain this status? What are the arguments for and against making it a state?

- Some people think Washington, D.C., should be made a state. Do you agree or disagree? Why isn't Washington, D.C., a state now?

- What rights and privileges do the residents of Puerto Rico and Washington, D.C. have now? What rights don't they have that residents of the states have?

Section 4.

Research/Discussion

This section guarantees that the national government will make sure that each state has elected leaders and that the national government will also respect state governments. It also says the federal government can send in armed forces when there are riots or other violent disturbances in a state.

- This section of Article IV reinforces part of the Constitution's system of "checks and balances." What is the system of checks and balances? How does this section work within that system?

Essay

This research question can be used as an essay assignment or a springboard for class discussion.

- The federal government has sent troops into states to stop riots and prevent looting after natural disasters. Find one historical or recent example of the use of troops to help maintain control after a disaster and write about it in an essay. What happened that caused National Guard troops to be used in a state in this case? Who called out the troops, the governor or the president? What happened when the troops were called out? Did the troops make the situation better or worse? Why?

Article V

Role play

Over the years, more than 7,000 amendments to the Constitution have been proposed to Congress. Of these, 33 passed through Congress and 27 were ratified, or approved, by the states. The proposed amendments have included everything from naming the U.S. "the United States of Earth" to the prohibition of divorce. In the past decade or so, issues involving school prayer, flag burning, abortion, and gun control have all been proposed as amendments.

Have one or more members of the class write an amendment. Ideally, the amendment should be about an issue that the class can relate to, that will stir debate, and can't be easily adopted or rejected. Some possible topics for your class's amendment include school prayer, metal detectors at the school door, and banning flag burning. After your class's amendment is written, divide the class into three groups: the Senate (smallest group), the House of Representatives (largest group), and the states. Next, the amendment should be debated separately by each of the three groups. After the debates, each group should take a vote on the amendment. A two-thirds majority is needed for the amendment to pass each house of Congress. If it passes both houses, three-fourths of the states need to approve the amendment in order for it to be ratified. This exercise isn't exactly the same as the amendment procedure outlined in the Constitution, but it should give the class an idea of how difficult it is to amend the Constitution.

After the vote, discuss the following with the class:

- Why do you think the framers made it so difficult to amend the Constitution?

- Why do you think approval by three-fourths of the states is needed to ratify an amendment while only two-thirds of each part of Congress need to approve the amendment to send it on to the states?

- Article V also outlines a procedure for a constitutional convention. With this procedure, the states could bypass the national government and pass amendments without the approval of Congress. There has never been a constitutional convention like this. Why do you suppose that is? Why do you think the framers put this procedure into the Constitution?

Essay

- Learn about a real proposed constitutional amendment that didn't pass, and write a brief essay that explains what the proposed amendment was, why it was supported, why it was defeated, and how you might vote on it.

- Article V says that each state will have an equal number of votes in the Senate and that this structure for the Senate cannot be amended. Why do you suppose the founders wanted to make sure that each state retained two votes in the Senate?

- The other section in this article that can't be amended has to do with slavery. What is the historical background for this part of Article V? What happened after 1808, when the rules against amending these slavery sections ended?

Article VI

Research/Discussion

This article contains the "supremacy clause," which many experts call the "linchpin of the Constitution." They say that without this clause, the entire document — and the nation — would fall apart. The supremacy clause says the Constitution is the supreme law of the land. It says that when national laws are in conflict with state laws, the national laws are superior. It also says that a national law has to abide by the Constitution in order to be valid.

This seems simple enough, but through the years this clause — and questions about its scope — have sparked many Supreme Court cases. Several such cases have asked whether federal agencies are akin to the national government in their dealings with the states. Often, the Supreme Court has found in favor of the agencies, which can overrule some state laws.

Divide the class into five groups and have each group do research on the one of the following federal agencies:

- The Environmental Protection Agency, or EPA.
- The Drug Enforcement Agency, or DEA.
- The Department of Transportation, or DOT.
- The Bureau of Alcohol, Tobacco and Firearms, or ATF.
- The Food and Drug Administration, or FDA.

Have each group research and answer the following questions about its agency:

- What is the purpose of this agency?
- How does it deal with state and other units of government?
- Does it have the power to overrule state or local laws? If so, when?
- Has it ever come in conflict with state or local units of government? If so, when?

Have the groups present their findings to the class. After the presentations, discuss the following questions:

- Which of these agencies do you think do a good job and which do you think don't do a good job? Explain your answers.
- Do you think it is right or fair that federal agencies can sometimes tell a state or other unit of government what to do? Why or why not?

Discussion

- During the Constitutional Convention, the framers debated how strong the states and the national government should be. They also debated the rights of both the states and the federal government. How does this article support either side of this debate?

- Why do you think that national and state officials must swear an oath to support the Constitution over any other law?

- Why do you think the framers said that it would go against the Constitution to favor one religion over another in filling federal offices? Do you think this part of the Constitution is needed today? Why or why not?

Article VII

Research/Discussion

The Constitution was written and agreed to by the framers on September 17, 1787. It was not ratified by the necessary nine states until July of 1788. In those ten months, many arguments about the new Constitution took place. As a class project, assign students to find out why the states had so many problems approving the Constitution. As part of their research, have students answer the following questions:

- Which state or states objected most to the Constitution? Why did these states object?

- How were these objections overcome?

- What were *The Federalist Papers*? Who wrote them and what did they say?

- Why did the framers want state conventions to ratify the Constitution instead of state legislatures?

- How was the first president, George Washington, chosen?

Have the students present their findings to the class. Then discuss the following questions:

- Why do you think the framers did not include an article stating the rights of the individual in the Constitution?

- Why do you think the states approved the Constitution when they knew it meant they would have to share power with the federal government?

Boston Massacre

Activities for the Amendments

NOTE TO TEACHER

These activities will help your students better understand what each of the amendments to the Constitution means. We suggest that students have a copy of the amendments you want to cover. The annotated amendments are printed elsewhere in this resource book.

The activities for the amendments include discussion questions, research/discussion questions, role plays, and essay questions. We encourage you to adapt any or all of these elements for your own use. For example, in many cases essay questions can also be used as class discussion questions, and vice versa.

Activities for the Amendments

 First Amendment: Freedom of Religion, Speech, and Press; the Right to Assemble and Petition the Government

Some people believe this amendment may be the single most important part of the entire Constitution. The First Amendment acts as a brake on the government and guarantees citizens several vital rights.

Discussion

- Why do you suppose "Congress" is the first word in this amendment?
- Why do you think the freedoms stated in the First Amendment are important?
- Are there limits to these freedoms? If so, what are they? Do you think these freedoms can ever be harmful or undesirable?
- Do you think these rights can ever be in conflict with each other? If so, give some examples of situations in which this kind of conflict might come up.
- Are there appropriate and inappropriate ways of exercising freedom of speech?

Research/Discussion

- The First Amendment guarantees freedom of the press. However, there are still restrictions on the press. What are they? Do you think these restrictions are in conflict with the First Amendment? Why or why not?
- The First Amendment distinguishes between forbidding laws that establish religion and the freedom to exercise religion. What is the difference between the two? Why do you think the framers made this distinction?
- The First Amendment guarantees the freedom of the public to assemble. What does this mean? Identify instances when assembly might not be allowed and explain why that might be.
- What is the freedom "to petition the government for redress of grievances"? Why do you suppose the First Amendment guarantees this right?

Essay

- Explain why the framers of the Constitution thought each particular right and freedom in this amendment was important. What happened in colonial America or in the early national period that led the country's leaders to add these freedoms to the Constitution?

- Describe which of the freedoms in the First Amendment is most important to you and why. Then discuss which of the freedoms is least important to you.

- The idea of "separation of church and state" comes from the First Amendment. In a brief essay, explain what this idea means and tell why you suppose the founders thought it was important. What is your opinion about the separation of church and state? Explain whether you feel it is important.

- Some historians say the Bill of Rights is similar to the state of Virginia's Declaration of Rights. Read both documents and write an essay explaining some of their differences and similarities. Do you think one of the documents guarantees more freedom than the other? Explain.

 Second Amendment: The Right to Keep and Bear Arms

The Second Amendment is the source of great controversy. The controversy centers on the interpretation and application of the amendment in today's United States. Did the writers of this amendment intend that every American should be allowed to own any type of gun? Or did the framers intend that the nation's military be made up of "citizen soldiers" who alone had the right to keep and bear arms? Are the framer's intentions relevant today, whatever they were?

Class debate

Select two groups from the class. One group will argue that every person is entitled to any type of gun without any restrictions. The other group will argue in favor of strict gun control measures. Each group should come up with well-reasoned arguments to support its position after doing research to answer the following questions:

- Why did the Constitution's framers feel that the right to keep and bear arms was important enough to be in the Bill of Rights?

- What happened in the early days of the United States that made people think this was an important issue?

- What sorts of arms were the framers talking about? Should the fact that arms technology has changed immensely since 1791 alter the interpretation of this amendment?

- Is the right to keep and bear arms still necessary today?

After the groups complete their research, stage a class debate on the Second Amendment. In the debate, students from each group should address each of the questions listed above.

Discussion

- What does "militia" mean, as the word is used in the Constitution?
- What do you think the Constitution's framers meant by a "well-regulated militia"?
- Why was a well-regulated militia necessary for the security of the nation?

Essay

- The National Rifle Association, or NRA, has led the way in resisting gun control laws. Research the NRA and write about its beliefs. What is the group's position on gun ownership? What are some of the controversies the group has been involved in?

- Some people believe the Second Amendment says you have to be a member of a militia in order to have the right to keep and bear arms. Others say the amendment's wording makes clear that anyone, not just members of the National Guard or other governmental military organization, has the right to keep and bear arms. What do you think the Second Amendment means? Expalin.

Third Amendment: Limits on Housing Soldiers

Discussion

Quartering soldiers in the homes of civilians isn't an issue today — or is it? As a class, discuss whether the Third Amendment is still needed. If it isn't, should it be taken out of the Constitution? Or should it be left in as a safeguard? Can anyone think of a situation in which the amendment might be important?

Discuss the following questions with your class:

- Some people say it is the duty of citizens to house members of the armed services. Do you agree or disagree?

- What does the Third Amendment suggest to you about how the framers of the Constitution viewed an individual's home?

Research/Discussion

- What happened prior to 1791 that made the Constitution's framers feel this amendment was important enough to make it part of the Bill of Rights?

Essay

- Imagine that you live in Boston in 1784. Soldiers who have just fought for the nation's independence need a place to live for a while and demand that you put them up in your house. Write a letter to your local political leader proposing a law that forbids soldiers from being quartered in people's homes without the owners' permission. Make sure that you clearly explain why this law is necessary.

- Some people say the less the Constitution is amended, changed, or otherwise edited, the stronger it will remain. Others say the Constitution contains old-fashioned wording and outdated parts that should simply be taken out. They say that keeping the Constitution up-to-date will make it stronger. Which side do you agree with more? Why?

 Fourth Amendment: Limiting Searches, Seizures, and Warrants

Amendments Four through Eight address the rights of citizens in connection with the law and the government. The Fourth Amendment has been linked to "right to privacy" cases. However, the specific words "right to privacy" cannot be found in any part of the Constitution. Fourth Amendment cases that reach the Supreme Court generally center on the right to privacy, what "unreasonable search and seizure" is, or what "probable cause" to search and seize is.

Discussion

Divide the class into five groups. Each group should take one of the following scenarios and come up with a list of reasons to permit and reasons not to permit the searches that are described. Each group should also decide if the search described is constitutional and explain why it is or is not. Group members should decide if they support or oppose the actions in the scenarios. Have each group present its findings to the class. Then have the rest of the class ask questions about the scenarios.

- *Sobriety checkpoints* — The police stop traffic to randomly check if drivers are under the influence of alcohol. Stopped motorists must submit to tests or they are held in jail. Those found under the influence are arrested.

- *Drug testing* — As a condition for being allowed on sports teams, high school athletes agree to be randomly tested at any time for illegal drug and alcohol use. Those who test positive are expelled from their sports and face suspension from school.

- *Traffic stops by police* — Young people and persons of color driving in a medium-sized city are routinely stopped by police. The police say these routine stops often lead to the arrest of lawbreakers, including people for whose arrest the police have an outstanding warrant and people carrying concealed weapons and drugs.

- *Screening for guns in school* — Schools set up metal detectors to scan for guns, knives, and other weapons. People who are found carrying weapons are subject to suspension and prosecution.

- *Caller ID* — Telephones come with an attachment that reveals a caller's identity. Callers do not have to give their permission to be identified, and they don't know that the person they are calling has Caller ID.

Discussion

- What do you think an "unreasonable search" is? Give some examples of searches you think are reasonable and unreasonable.

- Why do you think the Fourth Amendment was considered important enough to be included in the Bill of Rights?

- The Fourth Amendment is considered by some experts to be the "privacy amendment." That is, legal experts often use the Fourth Amendment when they argue that a person has the constitutional right to privacy, even though that right isn't specifically stated anywhere in the Constitution. Do you see the basis for the unwritten right to privacy in this amendment? If so, where? If not, why not? Do you think people have the right to privacy? If so, when? Do you think there are times when people don't have this right? If so, when?

Essay

- What is a warrant? What is the procedure the police have to go through to get one? Do you think this procedure is good or bad — that is, does it stand in the way of justice, or is it an important protection for the individual from the police?

- Under some circumstances, evidence collected by law enforcement officers cannot be used in court against a person charged with a crime. This is called the "exclusionary rule." Under this rule, judges can keep out or exclude certain evidence from court proceedings. Research some court cases and, in an essay, show some circumstances that would lead a judge to use the exclusionary rule. Do you think the exclusionary rule is good or bad? Why?

- The roots of the Fourth Amendment go back to the Magna Carta, the first English document that limited the power of the king or queen. In this country, searches and seizures by English troops helped spark the American Revolution. Do historical research to trace the growth of the individual's right to be protected from unreasonable searches and seizures.

 Fifth Amendment: Clarifying the Rights of the Accused

Role play

The grand jury system that was set up in the Fifth Amendment was put in place to protect the rights of the individual against the government. A grand jury consists of 12 to 23 citizens who are called upon to decide if there is enough evidence to charge one or more persons with a crime. Usually, grand juries sit for a specific amount of time and hear many cases. The jurors' names are kept secret and there are no news reports of what goes on during these hearings. In most grand juries, no judge is present. Jurors are free to ask witnesses questions, but most questions are asked by prosecuting attorneys. Witnesses who appear are not allowed to have their attorneys present in the hearing room, although their attorneys can wait outside. Witnesses are sworn to tell the truth, and if it is discovered that they haven't, they can be charged with perjury, or lying under oath. If a grand jury finds there is enough evidence to prosecute one or more people, the prosecuting attorney presents the findings to a judge and asks that the person or persons be charged with a crime.

For this exercise, divide the class into the following groups: jurors, one or more prosecuting attorneys, one or more defense attorneys, and a number of witnesses — including those testifying for the prosecution and those the prosecutors are investigating. Then have the groups consider one or more of the following scenarios in a mock-grand jury proceeding. The jurors who are selected should vote on whether charges should be brought against any of the accused. The prosecuting attorneys should begin the exercise knowing some of the questions they want to ask. The defense attorneys' role is to advise their witness-clients about what will take place before the jury and about how to answer questions. Remember, the defense attorneys may not be with their clients when the clients are questioned by the jury.

Scenarios:

- *A fallen bridge* — A bridge has collapsed in the city, causing many injuries. Inspectors say the bridge was built with faulty materials and in an unsafe manner. The bridge builder denies doing anything wrong and says the bridge was built according to what the city specified. The district attorney suspects that either the builders of the bridge bribed one or more city officials in order to cut corners and save money, or city officials somehow took money from the project without the builders' knowledge. Witnesses to be called: construction company owners, one or more city officials, inspectors.

- *A drug ring* — Police investigate a sharp increase in the amount of illegal drugs entering the city. Informants tell them two people are the masterminds behind the increase. The informants are also involved in illegal drugs and face jail time. Witnesses to be called: police officers, two or more informants, two suspects.

- *An assisted suicide* — A terminally-ill person dies after being injected with a lethal dose of drugs. The spouse of the dead person freely admits injecting the drugs to end the misery and pain the ill person was experiencing. The spouse then refuses to talk any further about what happened. The spouse faces a possible charge of murder. The district attorney wants to know where the spouse got the drugs for the injection. The attorney suspects that doctors or other medical personnel at the hospital where the terminally-ill person spent a lot of time supplied the spouse with the drugs. Witnesses to be called: one or more medical experts, one or more hospital employees, the spouse.

After the exercise is completed, discuss the following questions with the class:

- Do you think the grand jury system protects the rights of the citizen against the government? Why or why not?

- Do you think the grand jury system should be changed in any way, or should it be left as it is? If you think it should be changed, what changes would you make? If you think it should be left as it is, why do you think this way?

Research/Discussion

Divide the class into five groups and assign each group a clause of the Fifth Amendment. Make each group responsible for researching its clause and finding out what it means and why the framers of the Constitution might have thought this protection was important enough to include in the Bill of Rights. After the groups have finished their research, they should present their findings to the entire class for discussion.

Discussion

- What is a "capital, or otherwise infamous crime"?

- You sometimes hear about the Fifth Amendment in news reports on congressional hearings because someone has "taken the Fifth." What does this expression mean, and, specifically, which part of the amendment does it refer to?

- The Fifth Amendment contains a clause called the "double jeopardy" clause. Explain what double jeopardy means and identify the double jeopardy clause in this amendment.

Essay

- The purpose of the Fifth Amendment is to protect the rights of the accused. Do some research to find specific examples of events, practices, and abuses of the rights of the accused from the 17th and 18th centuries that the authors of the Bill of Rights wanted to get rid of.

- Explain how the Fifth Amendment protects the rights of people accused of crimes.

- The Miranda warning is something that every police officer making a felony arrest is required to read to the accused. It lists four specific rights, including the right to remain silent. This requirement became law after a 1966 Supreme Court case, *Miranda v. Arizona*. Research this case and write an essay explaining why you believe that the requirement either promotes constitutional rights or needlessly hampers police who are doing their duty.

- "The privilege against self-incrimination is one of the great landmarks in man's struggle to make himself civilized," wrote a former Harvard Law School Dean in reference to the Fifth Amendment. What do you think this statement means? Do you agree or disagree with this statement? Why?

- The process whereby a unit of government takes property from a citizen in order to use the property for something else is called "eminent domain." Eminent domain is used to take private property away from individuals to build roads, buildings, and other public structures. The citizen gets some protection from eminent domain in the Fifth Amendment: the state has to pay him or her for the property it takes. Do you think the process of eminent domain is fair or unfair? Why? Why do you think a protection against eminent domain was put in the Fifth Amendment?

# Sixth Amendment: Clarifying Rights in Criminal Cases

Discussion

The Sixth Amendment was written to protect the rights of an accused person during an actual criminal trial. The following activity is designed to illustrate what might happen if those rights did not exist.

Divide the class into eight groups and assign each group one of the rights in the Sixth Amendmentis listed here:

1. speedy trial
2. public trial
3. impartial jury
4. trial located in the area where the crime was committed
5. letting the defendant know what he or she is accused of
6. letting the defendant question prosecution witnesses
7. letting the defendant call defense witnesses
8. letting the defendant have a lawyer

Each group should learn as much as possible about one of these rights. Why did the framers think it was important to have a public trial? Why is it necessary to be able to question witnesses? And so on. Then each group should consider what would happen if their right was not part of the Sixth Amendment. Have each group present to the class an explanation of what its right means and what might happen if an accused person didn't have that particular right.

After the presentations, discuss the following questions:

- Is there one right that is more important than all the others in the Sixth Amendment? If so, what is it, and why is it most important?

- Is there a right in the Sixth Amendment that isn't as important as the others? If so, what is it, and why is it least important?

- Do you think there are any rights that should be added to the Sixth Amendment? If so, what are they?

- Why do you think the framers of the Constitution placed all these rights together in the Sixth Amendment?

Essay

- Some people think the trial process in criminal cases takes too long these days. Examine newspaper reports about one criminal trial in your area. What was the trial about? How long did it take to pick a jury and hold the trial? What was the verdict? Do you think the trial went on too long? Why or why not? Do you think that in general, trials go on too long? If so, is there anything you would change about our justice system to solve this problem? If not, why not? Are there any parts of the Sixth Amendment you would change? Be sure to use specific examples of court cases to back up your opinions.

- Write a speech to give to people who are moving to America about how the Sixth Amendment guarantees an impartial trial by jury to all accused people. Focus your speech on why a trial by jury is important to the American justice system. Give examples of what would happen without this Sixth Amendment protection. Don't forget to put in your speech any criticisms or concerns you might have about the jury system.

Seventh Amendment: Clarifying Rights in Civil Cases

Research/Discussion

Divide the class into two groups. One group should do research to find out what a civil case is and what its requirements are. The second group should do the same for criminal cases.

After the groups present their findings to the class, discuss the following questions:

- What are the differences and similarities between civil and criminal cases?

- It sometimes happens that criminal and civil cases intersect. That is, if someone is put on trial for a crime, he or she might also be sued by the crime's victim or the family of the crime's victim in civil court. In a famous example, the former football player O.J. Simpson was charged with the murders of his ex-wife and a man named Ronald Goldman. Mr. Simpson was found not guilty by a jury in criminal court. But then the family of Ronald Goldman sued Mr. Simpson in civil court and won. The jury in the civil trial found that Mr. Simpson was "responsible" for Mr. Goldman's death. From what you know about the differences between civil and criminal cases and how they're judged, how is it possible that Mr. Simpson could be found not guilty in a criminal trial and still found "responsible" for the crime in a civil case? Do you think it's fair that a person can face two trials for the same crime in this manner? Why or why not?

Discussion

- The Seventh Amendment says that in order for a civil case to be tried by a jury in a federal court, there must be more than $20 at stake. In 1791, this sum was more than a month's income for the average person. Do you think this amendment should be changed to reflect the change in economic times? Why or why not? If you think the amendment should be changed, what should the minimum amount required for a jury trial be? Why?

- What do you think the phrase "no fact tried by jury shall be otherwise reexamined in any court of the United States" means? How does this phrase compare with a similar clause in the Fifth Amendment? Do you think this phrase should govern cases in which a person is charged in separate criminal and civil actions for one event? Why or why not?

Essay

- Why did the framers of the Constitution put a minimum dollar value on civil cases that are guaranteed to receive a trial by jury? Why do you think they didn't offer a trial by jury to everyone?

- Today, a jury is often required to sit for months while it hears testimony in civil suits between businesses in federal court. These cases are often filled with technical discussions that are difficult for the average person to understand. Former Chief Justice Warren Burger wrote that the practice of using a jury in corporate civil trials "borders on cruelty." Juries are not always required in state civil court cases. Do you think there should be a change in the Seventh Amendment so that juries would not be required to hear all civil cases that come to federal court, or do you think the system should stay the way it is? Explain your reasoning.

- Why did the framers of the Constitution think it was important to have jury trials for federal civil cases? In what ways has our world changed since 1791 that might make this part of the Seventh Amendment out of date? How is our world similar to the world of that time?

Eighth Amendment: Limiting Bails, Fines, and Punishments

Discussion

First, discuss each clause of the Eighth Amendment with the class. Some discussion questions might include the following:

- What is bail and why is it part of this amendment?

- When are people ordered to pay fines?

- What do you suppose "cruel and unusual punishment" is?

Then discuss the following scenarios and questions with the class:

- *A fatal crime* — A person has been charged with a crime in federal court. The crime involves the murder of two FBI agents. The accused has no permanent address and no one knows how much money, if any, he has available. The prosecutor asks the judge to deny bail, saying the accused will run if he's let out on bail. The accused's defense attorney says this is unfair under the Eighth Amendment. How would you rule if you were the judge? Is the denial of bail a violation of the Eighth Amendment? Under what conditions, if any, can judges refuse bail?

- *An unusual fine* — A local company's top officials have been found guilty of approving the dumping of poisonous chemicals into a river. Experts say the chemicals will affect the river for years to come. The officials are given short jail terms and the company is fined $1 million as a punishment. This is a record fine for a case like this. The company will also have to pay for the cleanup of the river. In her decision, the judge says she imposed this fine because the chemicals are very harmful and will be in the river for years. The lawyers defending the company call the $1 million fine unfair. They say the company is willing to pay for the river's cleanup. They say the company as a whole was not aware of what the officials were doing. They also say paying the fine could put the company out of business, causing many innocent people to lose their jobs. Do you think the fine is too high? Why or why not?

81

- *Some punishments —*

A person has been found guilty of driving under the influence of alcohol for the third time. The judge ruled that the driver can now only drive an automobile to go to work and from work. The judge also said that for the next five years, a sign must be attached to the driver's car that reads: "CAUTION: I HAVE BEEN CAUGHT DRIVING DRUNK THREE TIMES." The driver says that since the punishments have been put in place, the police are unfairly stopping his car and administering breathalyzer tests to him almost every day. Is this a cruel and unusual punishment? Why or why not?

A person has been caught with crack cocaine near a school. The person says the crack was for personal use and not for sale. Under automatic sentencing guidelines — that is, guidelines set by the state or federal government that don't allow a judge to use his or her own judgment in sentencing — this person must go to jail for ten years. Is this a cruel and unusual punishment? Why or why not?

A man on death row in a state prison has been found to be mentally defective — that is, insane. This man does not know the difference between what is right and what is wrong. The man murdered three people. He was found to be sane before his trial but became insane in prison. The governor says the death sentence will be carried out. Is this a cruel and unusual punishment? Why or why not?

Essay

- The Supreme Court has been asked many times to determine whether a punishment is cruel and unusual. Learn about one of these Supreme Court cases. Explain some of the details of the case and the court's ruling. Do you think the court ruled correctly? Why or why not? Some cases that you might consider include *Furman v. Georgia* (1972); *Ingraham v. Wright* (1977); *Stanford v. Kentucky* (1989).

- Imagine you are a prosecutor in a murder case. Write an argument for the judge explaining why you think an accused murderer should be refused bail. Make sure to explain why this request does not violate the Eighth Amendment.

Ninth Amendment: Clarifying the Rights of People

Discussion

What does the term "enumeration" mean?

What does the phrase "construed to deny or disparage others retained by the people" mean?

Which rights not stated in the Bill of Rights might be protected by the Ninth Amendment?

This amendment has been called a safety valve and an "all-purpose lifeboat in which litigants can hope to reach whatever safe harbor they seek." What do you suppose this means? Why do you think the Ninth Amendment is called a safety valve?

Essay

- The ninth amendment was written by James Madison, one of the main framers of the Constitution. Some members of Congress objected to the Bill of Rights without it. After this amendment was added, the Bill of Rights was passed. Do some research to find out why there were objections to the Bill of Rights and why Madison wrote this amendment.

- Along with the Fourth Amendment, the Ninth Amendment is used in many Supreme Court cases as a guarantee for a citizen's right to privacy. However, it was not until 1965 that the Supreme Court used the Ninth Amendment for this purpose. The Supreme Court case in which the Ninth Amendment was first used in this way was *Griswold v. Connecticut*. Research this case and explain why the Supreme Court used the Ninth Amendment to uphold the right to privacy in this instance. Then explain why you think the Ninth Amendment hasn't been used more often in privacy cases.

Tenth Amendment: Clarifying States' Rights

Discussion

The Tenth Amendment is sometimes known as the "reserved powers" amendment. It says that the individual states have powers that the Constitution does not either give to the federal government or forbid to the states. However, the Tenth Amendment does not draw a sharp line between the powers of the states and the powers of the federal government. And it does not clearly state what powers the states actually have. This has led to a number of disagreements between the states and the federal government. Many of the laws that most affect us — laws about marriage, schools, welfare, alcohol, and so on — differ in the various states. When state laws conflict with federal laws, the Supreme Court must determine which laws supercede the others.

Discuss the following scenarios with the class. Try to determine who has the power in each case: the states or the federal government.

- *Water rights* — A major city in the Midwest is draining water from Lake Michigan for its own use. The federal government says the city does not have the right to take the water because it belongs to the nation as a whole and also to the other states that border Lake Michigan. The city says it has the right to take the water from the lake because there's nothing in the Constitution that forbids a city from taking the water it needs. How would you rule in this case, for the city or the federal government? On what would you base your decision?

- *Child labor* — The federal government says that no one under 16 can work for wages, with very few exceptions. The government also says that no one under age 18 can work in a factory around dangerous machinery. The owners of several big companies challenge this law. The states where the companies do business have laws that say children over 14 can work for wages and those over 16 can work in factories. How would you rule in this case, for the companies or the federal government? On what would you base your decision?

- *States' rights* — The federal government passes a law making it illegal to separate people of different races in schools, restaurants, and other public places. Several states have laws calling for the separation of the races. The states object to the new federal law, saying there is nothing in the Constitution that gives Congress or anyone else the power to dictate whether the people of different races should be separate. The case is taken to the Supreme Court. How would you rule in this case, for the states or the federal government? On what would you base your decision?

- *The speed limit* — Congress passes a law saying it's illegal to drive over 55 miles per hour on any highway in America. Congress cites safety concerns as the reason for passing the law. If any state doesn't follow the law, it will not get federal money to take care of its highways. Several states protest, saying only they have the right to set speed limits on state highways. How would you rule in this case, for the states or the federal government? On what would you base your decision?

At one time or another, the Supreme Court has been asked to rule on cases like these. The court's findings have been inconsistent. For example, it ruled against the city of Chicago in that city's effort to divert water from Lake Michigan, but, at first, it favored the states on the issue of child labor laws. With the class, discuss the following questions:

- Do you think the Tenth Amendment could be rewritten to reduce the disagreements and confusion between the states and the federal government when it comes to writing laws? If you think the amendment should be rewritten, what would you add or take out of it?

- Why do you think the writers of the Bill of Rights included the Tenth Amendment?

- What is the idea behind states' rights? Is the idea valid?

- What powers do the states have that aren't listed in the Constitution?

- Do you think the states have a fair chance before the Supreme Court when they argue against a law made by Congress?

Essay

- When the United States was governed by the Articles of Confederation, the states were very powerful. The Articles said that every state kept "its sovereignty, freedom and independence, and every Power, Jurisdiction and Right, which is not by this confederation expressly delegated to the United States." How does this understanding of states rights differ from the one presented in the Tenth Amendment?

- Explain how the Tenth Amendment limits the power of the federal government. Give examples of situations in which it does so.

The Bill of Rights

The first ten amendments to the Constitution are called the Bill of Rights. They list the protections a citizen has against the federal government. Do you think the framers of the Constitution neglected any important rights? Would you add anything to or take anything out of the Bill of Rights?

11th Amendment: Limiting Law Suits Against States

Ratified in 1795

The 11th amendment passed after the Bill of Rights was ratified in 1791. It was proposed following a 1793 Supreme Court decision on a case in which the state of Georgia was sued in federal court for withholding money from the estate of a dead South Carolina man. Georgia agreed it owed the money, but the state argued it was exempt from being sued in federal court. The Supreme Court didn't see things that way and said Georgia had to pay. The Supreme Court based its decision on the provisions in the Constitution that allows a state to sue a citizen of another state in federal court, as sometimes happens in criminal cases. The Court said that because this is so, citizens had to be allowed the chance to sue the states in federal court, too.

Because the states were afraid of giving up any of their power to the federal government, the court's decision caused a storm of protest across the small nation. If the states were to be sued, they wanted to be sued in their own courts, not in federal court. Congress quickly wrote this amendment, which was passed by all the state legislatures. Since that time, however, the Supreme Court has ruled on many cases in which citizens have sued the states in federal court. For one thing, the 11th Amendment doesn't forbid the Supreme Court from reviewing, or looking over, cases that began in state court — and the Supreme Court has reviewed such cases hundreds of times. In addition, a person who wants to begin a lawsuit against a state in federal court usually sues some representative of that state, like the governor or the head of a prison or school board. By suing an individual, that citizen can, in effect, sue the state in federal court. Because the 11th Amendment doesn't forbid this kind of lawsuit, some important cases between citizens of a state and a different state have begun in federal court.

These loopholes make it seem in some ways that the 11th Amendment does the opposite of what it was originally intended to do. Some experts say the amendment was written and passed so quickly that the people who supported it couldn't foresee how the federal government — that is, the Supreme Court — could still easily hear or review state cases after the Amendment took effect.

Research/Discussion

Divide the class into four small groups.

- Have students in one group study the 11th Amendment and put it into their own words.

- Have one group research the background of the 11th Amendment. Why did the states fear the federal government in the 18th and early 19th centuries?

- Have one group find out what the term "states' rights" means. Are state's rights defined in the Constitution? Are they written into state law? When were states' rights a big issue on the national scene and why was the issue so important? How does states' rights figure into politics today?

- Have one group take a look at the 14th Amendment, which many experts say contradicts the 11th Amendment. Does the 14th Amendment make the 11th Amendment out of date? If so, why? If not, why not?

Each group should present its findings to the class. After the groups have made their presentations, discuss the following questions:

- Should the 11th Amendment be rewritten? As an exercise, rewrite it to give the states the power they originally wanted to have.

- Is the 11th Amendment still needed today? Why or why not?

- Do you think other parts of the Constitution override the 11th Amendment or make it out of date? Why or why not?

- Should the states fear the federal government? Why or why not?

Essay

- Why do you think states would want to stop citizens from another state from suing them?

12th Amendment: Electing the President and Vice President

Ratified in 1804

Discussion

Have students read the bulleted points below that summarize the 12th Amendment, or read the summary aloud to the class.

- Electors meet in their own states and cast two separate votes — one for president and one for vice president.

- At least one of the candidates must come from a different state than the electors' own.

- Each state must count its electors' votes for president and vice president and transmit the totals to the president of the United States Senate.

- Each state's votes for president and vice president must be counted by the president of the Senate in front of the members of the House of Representatives and the Senate.

- The person who receives more than half of the total number of electoral votes for president is elected president.

- If no one receives more than half of the votes, the three candidates who receive the most votes for president are put on a ballot and voted on in the House of Representatives. Each state is allowed only one vote. In order for this election to be held, representatives from at least two-thirds of all the states must be present. The person who receives votes from more than half the states is elected president.

- If no one receives votes from a majority of the states, the representatives vote again and keep voting until they elect a president.

- If by March 4 (Inauguration Day, later changed to January 20) the representatives fail to elect a president, the vice president-elect shall act as president.

- The person who receives more than half of all the states' electoral votes for vice president is elected vice president.

- If no one receives a majority of the votes, the two candidates who received the most votes for vice president are voted on, by ballot, in the Senate. Representatives from at least two-thirds of all the states must be present to vote. The person who receives votes from more than half of all the senators is elected vice president

- All vice presidents must be constitutionally eligible for the office of the president.

Then discuss the following:
- Why do you suppose electors can't vote for more than one candidate from their own state?

- What are the constitutional requirements for a person to be vice president?

- Who elects the president if no candidate gets more than half of the electoral votes?

- Who elects the vice president if no candidate gets more than half of the electoral votes?

Essay

- The election of 1800 between Thomas Jefferson and John Adams led to the writing and ratification of the 12th Amendment. Do research on this election. What happened during this election? Why did Congress think it was necessary to amend the Constitution because of it?

- Why was the electoral college system set up by the framers of the Constitution? Why aren't the president and vice president elected by popular vote? Do you think the electoral college is still meaningful and useful today? Why or why not?

- The House of Representatives has twice elected the president. When did this happen and who were the candidates involved? What were the circumstances that led to these elections in the House?

- Compare Article II of the Constitution with the 12th Amendment. Describe how the rules for electing the president and vice president were changed.

13th Amendment: Ending Slavery

Ratified in 1865

Research/Discussion

The 13th, 14th, and 15th Amendments were proposed and ratified in the aftermath of the Civil War and were direct responses to war issues. In this exercise, students learn about how the Civil War was, in part, a defense of the Constitution. Divide the class into three groups. Each group should consider one of the following three issues, all of which were important in the war in terms of the Constitution:

slavery

states' rights

secession from the Union

Each group should think about which parts of the Constitution that are important to its topic were in question during the war. Why was slavery considered a controversial constitutional issue? Why did so many feel that the states that seceded had rebelled against the Constitution? Why did the states that seceded think they had the right to form their own confederacy? Each group should focus on both the North's and South's constitutional arguments for their actions during the war. When the groups are done researching, they should present their findings to the class and answer questions about its conclusions.

Discussion

- What is slavery?

- What does "involuntary servitude" mean?

- When does the 13th Amendment say it is all right to keep someone in involuntary servitude?

- What does "abolition" mean?
- In ten words or fewer, what is the main point of the 13th Amendment?

Essay

- How did the Union get the former slave states to ratify the 13th Amendment?
- Why was this amendment necessary even after President Lincoln had issued the Emancipation Proclamation in 1862?
- If the northern states had not required the southern states to ratify this amendment, do you think the southern states might have ever supported it on their own? Why or why not?

14th Amendment: Expanding the Rights and Protections of Citizens

Ratified in 1868

The first ten amendments — the Bill of Rights — were written to protect a citizen's rights against actions by the federal government. The 14th Amendment guarantees that a citizen's rights can't be trampled on by the states. That makes the 14th Amendment very important — some experts believe it is the most important amendment to the Constitution. These experts point out that the "due process" clause of the 14th Amendment says that all of the protections a citizen has from the federal government under the Bill of Rights are also protections from the states. Over the years, the Supreme Court has used the 14th Amendment to extend almost all the rights in the Bill of Rights to citizens suing states. In addition, the "equal protection" clause of this amendment has been used in dozens of civil rights cases brought against the states.

Research/Discussion

Divide the class into two groups. Have one group examine the equal protection clause of the 14th Amendment and have the other group look at the due process clause. Each group should figure out what its clause means and list examples of how the clause is used as well as examples of times when it is not valid. Members of the groups should then present their findings to the class and answer questions about the clauses.

After the presentations, discuss the following questions:
- Do you believe that the due process clause guarantees, as one former justice wrote, "the essential dignity and worth of each individual"? Why or why not?
- "Due process" is also mentioned in the Fifth Amendment. How are the two due process clauses similar? How are they different?
- Do you think the writers of this amendment thought that it would be used in cases beyond those arising in the South after the Civil War? Why or why not?

- How many ways can you think of to interpret the words "due process of law" and "equal protection of the laws"?

- Because of the 14th Amendment, it is now recognized that states may grant more rights than does the federal Bill of Rights, but never fewer. Do you think this is necessarily a good thing? Why or why not? Do you think the 14th Amendment takes too many rights away from the states? If so, how?

Essay

- Some people consider the 14th Amendment to be an addition to the Bill of Rights. Explain the similarities and differences between the first ten amendments and the 14th Amendment.

- The first section of the 14th Amendment is in part a response to the 1857 Supreme Court ruling in the case of *Dred Scott v. Sandford*. This Supreme Court case also helped lead to the Civil War. Learn about this case and explain how it helped lead to the Civil War and how the 14th Amendment reversed the court's decision in the case.

- Why did the political leaders of the northern states insist that the federal government should enforce the right of male former slaves to vote?

- The 14th Amendment has been cited in two of the most important civil rights cases of the 20th century: *Brown v. Board of Education* and *Roe v. Wade*. Learn about one of these cases and explain how the 14th Amendment was used in the case you chose. Would the case have been decided differently if the 14th Amendment was not part of the Constitution?

- Today, the first section of the 14th Amendment is by far the amendment's most important part. When the 14th Amendment was passed, however, Congress thought the second section was equally important. It says that if any state stands in the way of qualified people voting, that state's representation in Congress could be cut. Do research to find out why Congress in 1866 wrote this section. Was the section ever enforced?

- The third section bars officials of the Confederacy from holding congressional or presidential office. What was the South's reaction to this section? Was this section ever overturned or revised?

15th Amendment: Legalizing African American Suffrage

Ratified in 1870

Research/Discussion

Like the 13th and 14th Amendments, the 15th Amendment is a Reconstruction amendment. Reconstruction refers to the period following the Civil War when the South was rebuilt, or reconstructed. Historians disagree about whether Reconstruction helped or harmed the South and the nation as a whole. The North wanted to bring the southern states back into the Union and grant former slaves their civil rights. At the same time, many people in the

North wanted to punish the South for starting the war. Most southern whites didn't want former slaves to be their equals under the law. The South also objected to people from the North holding government offices in the South. Southerners were especially bothered by black people voting and holding elected offices.

There were many plans for Reconstruction. In the following exercise, divide the class into groups to research these different plans. Each group should find out about the plan assigned to it and the problems that plan had. The groups should also keep in mind the roles the 13th, 14th, and 15th Amendments played in the plans.

After the groups have finished their research, hold a debate or a mock court in which the various plans' merits and demerits are pitted against each other.

The Lincoln Plan — President Lincoln wanted to pardon every southerner who took an oath to support the Union. New state governments would write new state constitutions that would abolish slavery. Congress added the 13th Amendment, which freed the slaves, to this plan and established the Freedmen's Bureau, which would "protect the interests" of freed slaves.

The Johnson Plan — Andrew Johnson, who took office after President Lincoln was killed, wanted to pardon all southerners except the Confederacy's leaders and rich supporters. New state governments would abolish slavery and the states themselves would figure out the role the freed slaves would have in government.

The Radical Republican Plan — This group thought that Congress, not the president and the executive branch, should make Reconstruction policy. The Radicals felt the South should be occupied by federal troops for a period of time so that the rights of freed slaves would be protected. They felt former slaves should be allowed to vote and hold public office because that would be the only way the new southern governments would remain loyal to the Union.

The Moderate Republican Plan — Moderate Republicans agreed with the Radicals that Congress should make Reconstruction policy and that federal occupation of the South should protect newly-freed slaves. They agreed with President Johnson that the states should decide if blacks should vote.

Using the research from their first part of this activity, students should discuss the following questions:

- Which of these plans do you favor the most? Which do you favor the least? Why?

- Why do you suppose the Radical Republicans wanted to make sure that all black men over 21 could vote?

- What happened when blacks were allowed to vote in the South during Reconstruction? Did they take over state governments? Which party's candidates did they vote for?

- What is the Ku Klux Klan? How did its rise during Reconstruction affect African Americans living in the South?

- What were the "black codes"? How did they affect the Reconstruction process?

- What were the "grandfather clauses"? How did they discriminate against black people?

- If the South had not resisted Reconstruction, do you think the 14th and 15th Amendments would have become part of the Constitution? Why or why not?

- What effect did the 13th, 14th, and 15th Amendments have on Reconstruction and on the South?

- What led to the end of Reconstruction? What happened to African Americans in the South after Reconstruction ended?

Essay

- Argument over Reconstruction policy led to the impeachment of President Andrew Johnson. In an essay, explain what impeachment is, how it happens, and why President Johnson was impeached. What happened during the impeachment hearings? Was the president convicted?

- During the Reconstruction era, blacks became members of Congress for the first time. Research one of the black men who was elected to office from the South during Reconstruction. How did this person become elected? How long did he serve? What happened to him after his election?

- Do research on Reconstruction and write an essay explaining whether you think the era helped or harmed the South. What do you think could have been done to help the South re-enter the Union and, at the same time, to protect the lives and rights of southern African Americans?

- What steps did the North take to bring about passage of the 13th, 14th, and 15th Amendments? How difficult or easy was it to pass these amendments? How did the South respond to the pressure for the passage of the amendments? What tactics or means did the South use to fight them?

16th Amendment: Income Tax

Ratified in 1913

Research/Discussion

Divide the class into four groups. Each group should research one of the following taxes or tariffs:

income tax

protective tariff

sales tax

property tax

Each group should find out what role its tax or tariff has played in the nation's history. When was the tax first used? What was it used for? What has been proposed over the course of the nation's history to either get rid of the tax or expand it? Has the tax been successful? If so, how? After completing their research, members of each group should present their findings to the entire class.

Following the presentations, discuss the following questions:

- Of the four taxes and tariffs you studied, which do you think is the most fair? Why? Which do you think is the least fair? Why?

- Do you think tariffs help or hurt a nation's economy? Why?

- Do you think the property tax should be used to fund schools? Why or why not? If you don't think it should be used, what should replace it as a source for school funding?

- Do you think sales taxes put more tax burden on richer or poorer people? Explain your answer.

Essay

- Why do you think the people and the state governments supported the creation of the income tax? How much was the first income tax? How much is the tax today for a person who earns $25,000 a year?

- This amendment allows for the collection of a tax that is called a "progressive income tax." What is a progressive income tax and how does it differ from a tax collected "in proportion to the census or enumeration," as defined in Article I, Section 9?

- What were some of the circumstances in the beginning of the 20th century that led to the creation of the income tax?

- This amendment overruled an 1895 Supreme Court ruling in the case of *Pollock v. Farmers' Loan and Trust*. Learn about this case and explain how the 16th Amendment directly changed the ruling in this case.

17th Amendment: Electing Senators Directly

Ratified in 1913

Research/Discussion

This amendment changed Article I, Section 3, of the Constitution. That section called for state legislatures to appoint their states' senators. This amendment calls for the direct election of senators by the states' citizens. The framers of the Constitution thought it was important that states have the power to appoint senators, which is why they didn't provide for the direct election of senators originally.

Have members of the class, either alone or in groups, research the following questions and report their findings to the entire class.

- Why did the framers of the Constitution want state legislatures to appoint senators instead of having senators elected by the people?

- Why did the members of Congress want to change the Constitution so that senators could be elected directly by the people? What was happening during this time that led to this amendment being passed by Congress and ratified by the states?

- Sometimes people compare the U.S. Congress with the two Houses of the English Parliament — the House of Commons and the House of Lords. Research how the members of England's Parliament are chosen. What are the similarities and differences between Congress and Parliament? Did the 17th Amendment do anything to make Congress and Parliament more alike or different?

- By the time this amendment was ratified, 29 states already had rules by which U.S. senators were elected directly by citizens. Why was an amendment needed to put into effect something that was already happening across the nation?

After members of the class give their reports, discuss the following questions:

- Do you think the framers of the Constitution made a mistake when they wrote that senators must be appointed by state legislatures? Why or why not?

- How do you think 29 states could get away with electing senators when it says in the Constitution that senators have to be appointed by state legislatures?

- Do you see any differences or similarities between how presidents and vice presidents are elected and how senators were elected before the 17th Amendment? If so, what are the similarities or differences?

18th Amendment: Prohibition

Ratified in 1919

Research/Discussion

All through America's history, the use of alcohol has been opposed by certain groups. During the first part of the 20th century, an increasing number of people believed that alcohol threatened the nation. In 1917, when Congress approved the 18th Amendment, many states, counties, and towns already had "dry laws" — laws that banned alcohol in that area. Pretend it is 1917 and the 18th Amendment is being debated. Divide the class into two groups — one group supports the ban on alcohol, the other opposes it. The members of each group should research and discuss the reasons for their position in the Prohibition debate. In formulating their reasons, the members of each group should act as if they are living during the Prohibition era, and consider the social and political issues of the era, as well as states' rights issues. Each group should then present its position to the class and be prepared to answer questions. You may want to set this activity up as a debate, in which each group presents its view in a limited amount of time, with additional time for rebuttal and questions. Then the class as a whole should vote on whether the 18th Amendment should be ratified.

Discussion

- Do you think Prohibition made sense when the 18th Amendment was ratified?

- Why do you suppose the writers of the 18th Amendment wanted it to take effect one year after ratification instead of right away?

Essay

- Write a report on what happened when Prohibition took effect. What happened in the country when it was no longer legal to buy or sell alcohol? Did Prohibition stop the use of alcohol?

- The 18th Amendment grew out of the temperance movement. What was the temperance movement? What were some of the beliefs the movement supported? Who were the leaders and followers of temperance? What happened to this movement after the amendment was passed?

- There are many stories about Prohibition enforcement. Describe three efforts made on the federal, state, or local level to prevent the production, sale, transportation, or consumption of alcohol. Were these efforts successful? Why or why not?

- The last section of this amendment requires a seven year time limit for ratification. The 18th Amendment was the first amendment with a time limit for ratification. Why do you think the writers of the 18th Amendment wanted a time limit? In your answer, explain some advantages and disadvantages of this time limit.

- Some people consider the 18th Amendment a violation of states' rights. Explain why someone might think that way. Do you agree with this position? Why or why not?

19th Amendment: Legalizing Woman Suffrage

Ratified in 1920

Research/Discussion

The passage of the 19th Amendment in 1920 was the biggest victory up to that time for women's rights in this nation. But even after the amendment's passage, many people in the United States still felt that women were not considered truly equal to men under the law. The growth of the women's rights movement in the 1960s led to a call for the Equal Rights Amendment to the Constitution. In 1972, Congress passed the Equal Rights Amendment, often called the ERA. It read:

Equality of rights under the law shall not be denied or abridged by the United States or any state on account of sex.

Congress required that the amendment be ratified by the necessary 38 states within seven years in order for it to become part of the Constitution. Congress later voted to extend the deadline by three years. By the 1982 deadline, only 35 states had ratified the amendment, so it failed to become part of the Constitution. Since 1982, the ERA has been reintroduced in Congress many times, but it has never again been passed.

Divide the class into four groups. The first group should research some of the reasons many felt that women still did not have equal rights with men after 1920. Some of the issues this group researches might include wages for men and women for the same jobs; jobs that could be held by men and not by women and vice versa; issues relating to women getting insurance, credit, and government benefits; and so on.

Another group should research the women's rights movement of the 1960s. How did it come into being? Who were its leaders and what were their goals? Why did the women's rights movement flourish at this time?

The third group should research the history of the Equal Rights Amendment in Congress. Who wrote it? When was it first introduced in Congress? Who introduced it in Congress? What problems did it face getting passed in Congress? Why did Congress extend the period for its ratification? Why has it been voted down in Congress since 1982?

The fourth group should research the controversies the surrounding the ERA and the struggle to get it ratified by the states. What were some of the arguments for its passage? What were some of the arguments for its defeat? Who opposed it? Who supported it? Which states ratified the amendment? Which states did not?

After the groups give their reports to the class, discuss the following questions:
- Why do you think the Equal Rights Amendment was passed by Congress?
- Do you think the ERA should have been ratified by the states? Why or why not?
- Do you think the ERA is needed today? Why or why not?

Discussion

- Why do you suppose women wanted the right to vote?
- Why do you suppose some people wanted to prevent women from voting?
- Nine states had already made it legal for women to vote in national elections when the 19th Amendment was passed. There was a growing movement in other states to allow women to vote. With this in mind, do you think the 19th Amendment was necessary? Why or why not?
- In 1920, after the 19th Amendment was ratified, which Americans had the right to vote and which did not have this right?

Essay

- In 1848, a group of women met in Seneca Falls, New York, and officially started the women's rights movement in the United States. Find out more about the Seneca Falls Convention. Then, in an essay, write about what happened there. How did the Seneca Falls Convention eventually lead to the women suffrage movement?

- From the time the Constitution was ratified, many women argued for the right to vote. Lucretia Mott, Elizabeth Cady Stanton, and Susan B. Anthony are three well-known leaders in the women suffrage cause. Carrie Chapman Catt, Lucy Burns, Alice Paul, and many others helped convince state legislatures of the importance of giving women the right to vote. Learn about one person or organization that worked for woman suffrage and write about the struggles that person or group faced. Who supported this person or group? What was the person or group's reaction when the amendment was finally passed?

20th Amendment: Clarifying Presidential and Congressional Terms

Ratified in 1933

Discussion

- Why do you think Congress is required to assemble at least once a year?
- What do you suppose could make a president-elect ineligible to take office?

Essay

- The 20th Amendment is referred to as the "lame duck amendment." It's called this because it reduced the amount of time an elected official who did not win a new term remained in office. In Congress, the time between an election and the date when new Congress members took office could stretch to 13 months. A lame duck president served a little over four months before the new president took over. What situations involving actions by lame duck presidents and members of Congress led to this amendment? What was the effect of the situation and actions on the nation?

21st Amendment: Repealing Prohibition

Ratified in 1933

Discussion

The 21st Amendment repealed, or reversed, a previous amendment, the 18th. The 18th Amendment prohibited the sale of "intoxicating beverages" — beer and liquor. Some people point to the 21st Amendment as proof that the government cannot "legislate morality." They say that laws passed to prevent people from harming themselves always fail. Others disagree, saying that the government has the responsibility to safeguard the nation's health. With this in mind, discuss the following situations as a class:

- Some people think all drugs should be legalized. They say this will put an end to the crimes associated with illegal drugs, both on the part of the people who supply drugs and those who use them. Those who think drugs should be legalized say the government would then be better able to regulate, or control, drugs and keep an eye on people who use them. What do you think of this proposal? Do you think making drugs legal would end the abuse of drugs in this country? Would you support or oppose a law legalizing all drugs? Explain your answers.

- The health hazards of smoking are well known. Studies show that if someone doesn't start smoking by the age of 18, he or she isn't likely to smoke at all. Federal and state governments want to stop young people from smoking. Some people say government programs to prevent smoking actually encourage young people to smoke because they make the act of smoking seem glamorously dangerous or rebellious. Do you agree or disagree? Why? Should governments try to stop young people from smoking? Why or why not? If you were in charge of the government, what, if anything, would you do to stop young people from smoking?

- Some state and local governments have motorcycle and bicycle helmet laws. Do you think any government has the right to make laws saying people have to wear helmets when they drive motorcycles or ride bikes? Why do you suppose the government cares if someone doesn't wear a helmet?

- Do you think the government should have some say in keeping people from harming themselves? How far should the government go in trying to keep people from harming themselves?

Essay

- When the 21st Amendment was passed in 1933 repealing Prohibition, it brought an end to a lawless era of "bootlegging" — making and selling illegal beer and liquor. Many people supported the repeal of Prohibition because Prohibition made lawbreakers of many otherwise law-abiding people. Supporters of the 21st Amendment also thought that Prohibition led many people to have less respect for the law in general. Do research on the Prohibition era. Do you think Prohibition encouraged disrespect for the law in general? Why or why not?

- The 21st Amendment didn't automatically make alcohol legal across the nation. It allowed states and even cities and counties to make their own laws. Some places remained "dry" — that is, they tightly controlled the sale of liquor or even made it illegal. Find out about one such place — either a state, city, or county. What kind of laws did the government of this area pass and enforce? Were the laws somehow bypassed by citizens within the area? If so, how were the laws bypassed? Is this place still "dry"? If so, what effect, if any, do laws prohibiting alcohol have on the area?

- The repeal of the 18th Amendment made most Americans happy. Why? Make sure that your answer takes into account the social and economic circumstances that many Americans were experiencing in the early 1930s when the 21st Amendment was passed.

- The 21st Amendment is the only amendment that repeals an amendment that had been previously passed. It is also the only amendment ratified by state conventions. What is the difference between state conventions and state legislatures? Why did the writers of this amendment say state conventions should be used to ratify it, rather than letting state legislatures decide if the amendment should be ratified? Why did Congress bypass state legislatures to get action on the amendment?

22nd Amendment: Limiting Presidents to Two Terms

Ratified in 1951

Research/Discussion

Select two groups of three or more people from the class. The people in one group are opposed to the 22nd Amendment. They believe that if the citizens of the United States want to elect someone to multiple terms as president, they should be free to do so. The other group supports the amendment. Members of this group believe that two terms is long enough time for one person to run the country. Both groups should come up with reasons and examples to support their positions to the class. Each group should make a brief presentation to the class stating the reasons for the group's position. You may also want to add time for rebuttal, so that the groups can answer each other's arguments. The rest of the class should be prepared to ask questions of both groups. Class members should then vote on which side of the debate they support.

Discussion

- When he was president, Ronald Reagan said he thought a president should serve only one term of six years. He said this would eliminate the campaigning any president who wants a second term has to do. He also said that if a president could not accomplish what he or she wanted to do in six years, that president would likely not be able to do so in eight. What do you think of Mr. Reagan's proposal? Do you favor it or oppose it? Why?

- Some people believe this amendment prevents the executive branch of government from becoming strong and centralized. Do you think this is true? Why or why not? Do you think it would be good or bad to have a strong, centralized executive branch? Why?

Essay

- Since the time of George Washington, presidents have — by tradition, not law — served only two terms. That tradition ended in 1940. Which president prompted the 22nd Amendment by serving multiple terms? Why did this president decide to run for a third and fourth term? What was the public reaction to his decisions? Why do you suppose there was strong support for this amendment in the late 1940s? What was happening when the amendment was proposed, and what were the public's reactions to and opinions about the amendment during this time?

23rd Amendment: Legalizing Suffrage in Washington, D.C. for Presidential Elections

Ratified in 1961

Research/Discussion

Washington, D.C., has more people than 13 of the 50 states, yet it only gets three electoral votes in presidential elections. It has no representation in Congress. Instead, someone speaks for the city to the members of Congress who oversee its government. Research how Washington, D.C., came into existence. Find out how Congress oversees Washington's government and how it works to solve the problems the city has. Then discuss the following questions:

- How did Washington, D.C., come into existence? Why was it named the nation's capital?

- How does the government of the capital work? Where does the city get its money? Who speaks for it before Congress? Who represents its interests?

- Until the 23rd Amendment was ratified, the citizens of Washington, D.C., were not allowed to vote in presidential elections. Do you think this restriction on voting was fair or unfair? Why do you think Washington is treated so differently from the states? Is this fair? Was the 23rd Amendment a good idea? Why or why not?

- Do you think the District of Columbia should have official representatives in Congress? Why or why not?

- Has the way the city is governed caused any problems for the people who live there? If so, what are some of these problems?

- Three cities have been the "seat of government of the United States." What were the cities, when was each of them the capital, and why were the first two replaced?

24th Amendment: Ending the Poll Tax in Federal Elections

Ratified in 1964

Another name for a poll tax is a "head tax." When a poll tax is in effect, people must pay a fee when they register in order to vote. The 24th Amendment, which ended poll taxes in federal elections, was passed by Congress in 1962 and ratified by the necessary number of states by 1964. The amendment was passed during the height of the civil rights movement of the 1950s and 1960s. In 1966, the Supreme Court barred the use of the poll tax in state and local elections.

Ever since America's colonial days, people often had to pay a tax or prove property ownership in order to vote. Many times, people who wanted to vote also had to prove they could read. The procedure they had to go through to prove this was called a "literacy test." Literacy tests were also struck down in federal court.

Essay

- Why were poll taxes common in the colonial era? Why were property owners the only people who were allowed to vote at this time? When did voting laws begin to change? How did they change? What happened in the U.S. to lead to this change?

- Poll taxes and literacy tests came to be a way to keep poor people from voting, especially in the South after the Civil War. In this way, poll taxes and literacy tests were part of the South's "Jim Crow" laws. What were Jim Crow laws? When did they come into being? When were they ended? How? Who favored these laws and who opposed them? Give some examples of these laws. How effective were they at keeping poor people, especially blacks, from voting?

- A big goal of the civil rights movement of the 1950s and 1960s was to find a way to defeat poll taxes and literacy tests and make it possible for African Americans to vote. Drives to get blacks registered to vote took place all across the South, but especially in Mississippi, Alabama, and Louisiana. Do research and report on one of these courageous voting drives. What problems did blacks face in registering? Who was involved in trying to get them registered? What are some of the things that happened during this time?

- Do research on how the 24th Amendment was written and passed by Congress and then ratified by the states. What was happening in Congress during this time? Who favored this amendment? Was there opposition to it? What happened as the amendment was debated, and how was any opposition defeated? Were there any states that did not ratify the amendment?

- In 1964, a group of civil rights workers tried to replace the regular Democratic Party delegates, or representatives, to the Democratic National Convention. Why did this group want to replace the regular delegates? What happened at the convention?

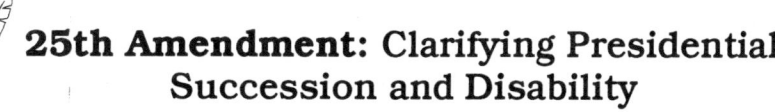

25th Amendment: Clarifying Presidential Succession and Disability

Ratified in 1967

Role play

Pretend that for the last few months, the president has been incapacitated by a heart attack or stroke. The president handed over duties to the vice president but now feels physically able to resume office. The vice president and more than half the cabinet disagree. Four or more students should play the roles of the president, the president's doctor or doctors, and two cabinet members — the Secretary of Defense and the Secretary of State — who agree that the president should resume office. They should make their arguments for the president based on the Constitution. Another three or more students should play the parts of the vice president, a cabinet member or members who think the president should not resume office, and one or more medical experts enlisted by the vice president for support. This group should think of sound reasons for the vice president to retain the office of the president. A third group, made up of the the rest of the class, should take the part of Congress. Congress should ask questions of both groups and then vote on whether the president should resume office.

After the role play activity, the class as a whole should discuss the following questions:

- What problems do you think could grow out of this amendment?

- What benefits does the amendment provide?

- What do you think could happen under this amendment if the president and vice president belonged to a political party different from that of the majority of members of Congress? What safeguards, if any, does the amendment put in place to prevent problems like this from happening?

Discussion

- What are the rules for filling the office of vice president when it becomes empty?

- List some reasons the president might need to write a letter to the leaders of Congress in order to pass his or her powers and duties on to the vice president.

Essay

- When were the offices of president and/or vice president vacant in the 70 years prior to the ratification of this amendment in 1967? What happened to cause these vacancies? How were they filled?

- Replacing an ill president for a period of time with the vice president is a touchy matter. Do research on the terms of Woodrow Wilson (second term), Dwight Eisenhower (first term), and Ronald Reagan (first term). How were these presidents' offices filled while they were incapacitated? In the case of the first two presidents, do you think the 25th Amendment would have been used if it had existed? Why or why not? During President Reagan's recovery, do you think the amendment should have applied? Why or why not?

- Between 1974 and 1976, the United States had both a president and a vice president who were not elected to office. In a brief essay, describe what happened during those years that led to this situation. How did the government deal with vacancies in the offices of president and vice president before the 25th Amendment? Give some examples of how vacant offices were filled. Based on your research, do you think the 25th Amendment was a good addition to the Constitution? Why or why not?

26th Amendment: Giving the Right to Vote to Citizens 18 Years or Older

Ratified in 1971

Research/Discussion

Divide the class into three groups. One group should argue that the voting age should remain 21 as the founders originally planned. Another group should argue that the voting age should be 18. The last group should argue that the voting age should be lowered to 16. Each group should come up with a list of reasons to back up its arguments. As they do their research, the groups should consider the social, cultural and political circumstances of the year the framers set the voting age at 21 (1787), the year this amendment we ratified (1971), and today.

When the groups have completed their research, each group should present its best case to the class. In addition, you may want to give each group time to rebut the arguments of the other groups. Once the groups have presented their cases, the rest of the class should be given the opportunity to question them.

After the debate, take a class vote to see what students think the voting age should be. Then discuss the class's decision as a group.

Discussion

- Why do you suppose the framers of the Constitution believed that voting must be done by informed and responsible citizens? Do you believe that 18-year-olds are informed enough to vote? Explain.

- Voter turnout in America is much lower than in many other nations. Why do you think this is so? Explain your answer.

Essay

- This amendment was passed in 1971 in 107 days — the shortest time for the ratification of any amendment. The Vietnam War played a big role in getting this amendment approved by Congress and passed by the states. After researching this era in history, explain the relationship between the Vietnam War and this amendment.

- More and more citizens have been given the right to vote since the nation's founding. Write a brief essay reviewing changes in voting rights. Consider many different groups in your essay, including African Americans, women, and Native Americans — who were given the right to vote in a 1924 law that also granted them citizenship. Conclude your essay by listing the groups that aren't allowed to vote in national elections. Do you think the remaining restrictions on voting are fair? Why or why not?

27th Amendment: Congressional Pay

Ratified in 1992

Discussion

Unlike the 26th Amendment, which was passed by Congress and the states in 107 days, the 27th Amendment took 203 years to ratify! The amendment was written in the 1780s as part of the original Bill of Rights. Although it was approved by Congress in 1789, only six of the necessary 11 states approved it at that time. In 1873, another state ratified it. Not until 1978 did another state approve the amendment. But in the 1980s and early 1990s, more states jumped on board, and in May of 1992, Michigan became the 38th state to approve this amendment, and the amendment became part of the Constitution — 203 years after it was first proposed.

With this information in mind, discuss the following questions. Some of them may require a bit of research.

- What is the concern this amendment addresses?

- Why do you suppose the framers of the Constitution wanted to put this amendment into the Bill of Rights, which, for the most part, talks about the rights of individual citizens?

- Why do you think it took so long to ratify this amendment?

- Why do you think so many states decided to approve this amendment in the 1970s, 1980s, and early 1990s? What was happening on the national scene at that time that led 30 states suddenly to pass the amendment?

- Some amendments have had seven-year deadlines for ratification. Obviously, there was no deadline at all for this amendment. Which do you think is better — having a deadline for states to ratify an amendment or not having a deadline at all? Give reasons for your answer.

Timeline

Timeline

TO PUT THE TIMELINE TOGETHER:

Cut out timeline segments along dotted lines. Match up letters on timeline ends (A to A, B to B, etc.). Tape or glue the ends together, overlapping them so that the dark strips on the ends of the sections are covered.

Then cut out the timeline icons (p.108) and place them on the timeline at or near the dates of their occurrence.

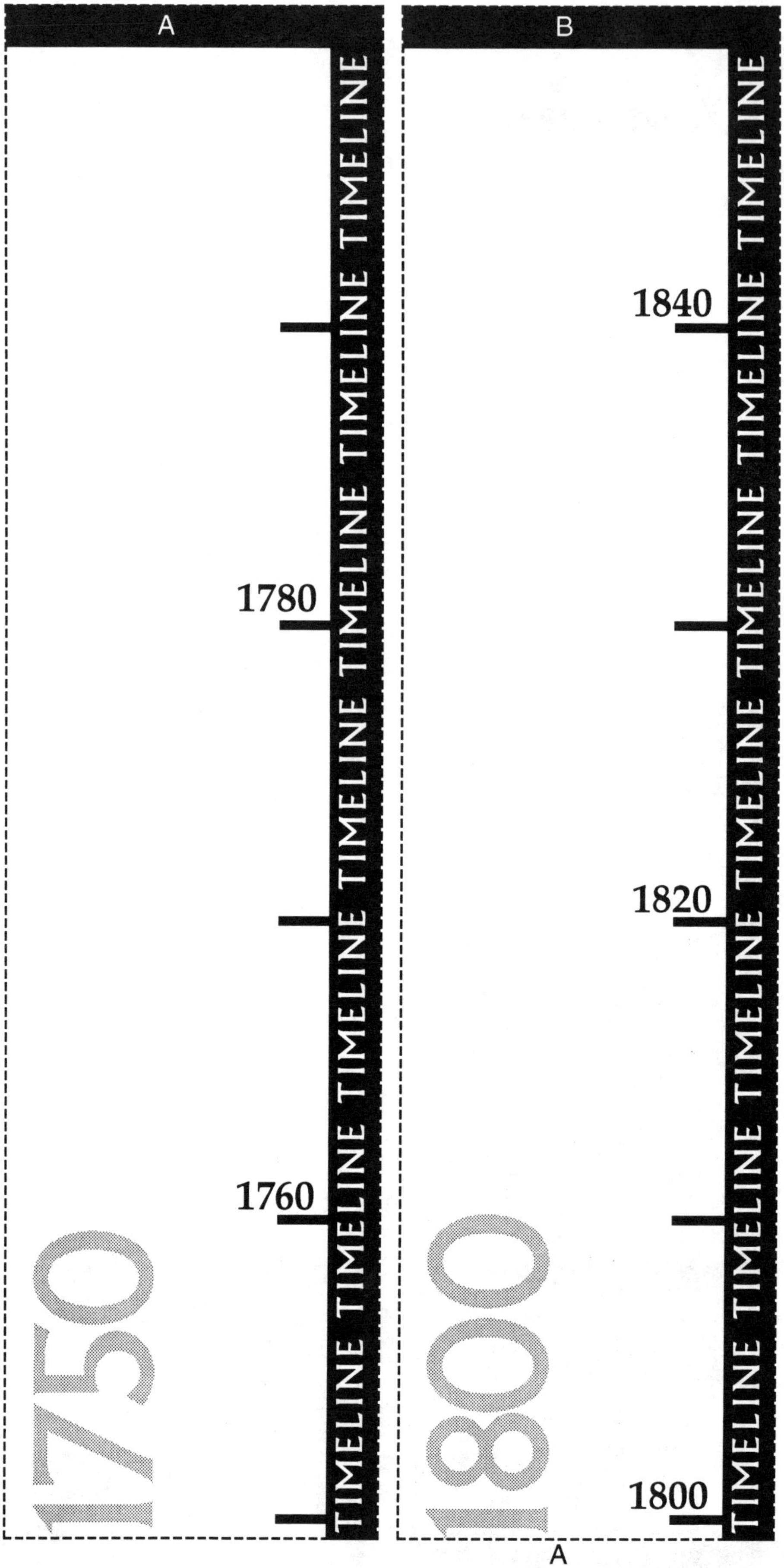

A

B

1840

1780

1820

1760

1750

1800

1800

A

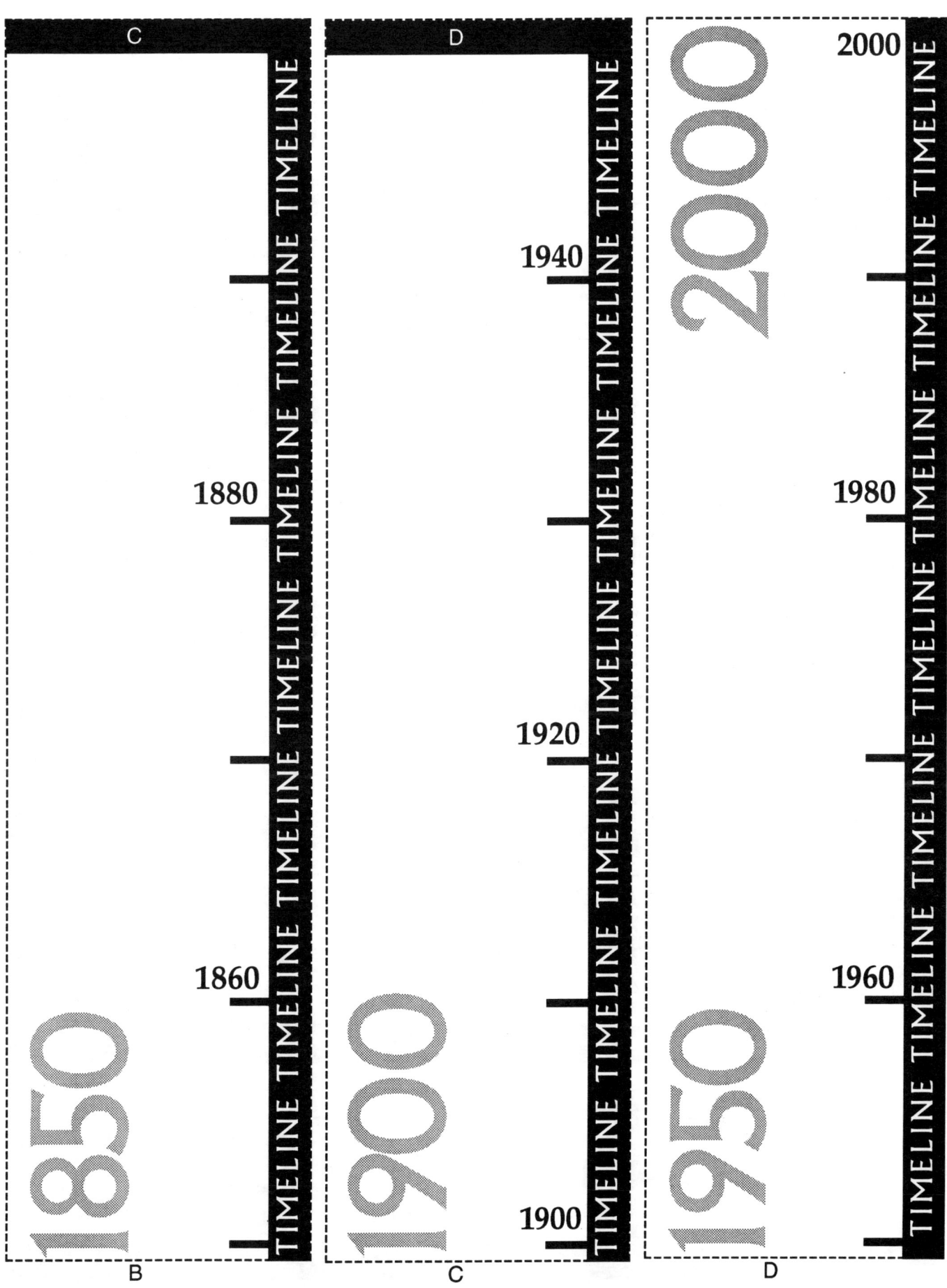

Timeline

These icons symbolize significant events in history. They should be placed on the timeline at or near the dates of their occurrence. You may also wish to add more events to the timeline

George Washington is elected president

Civil War begins

Constitutional Convention opens

Bill of Rights ratified

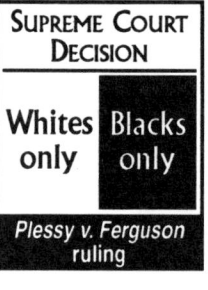
SUPREME COURT DECISION
Plessy v. Ferguson ruling

SUPREME COURT DECISION
Brown v. Board of Education of Topeka ruling

AMENDMENT 13
Slavery abolished

SUPREME COURT DECISION
Dred Scott v. Sandford ruling

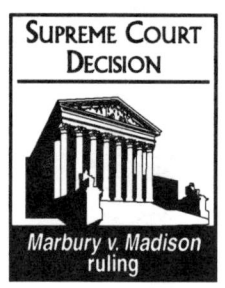
SUPREME COURT DECISION
Marbury v. Madison ruling

AMENDMENT 11
Limits suits among states

AMENDMENT 12
President and vice president chosen by electors

AMENDMENT 17
Senators popularly elected

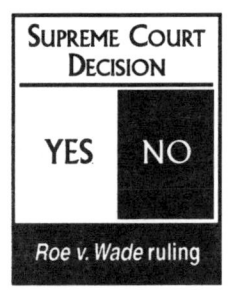
SUPREME COURT DECISION
Roe v. Wade ruling

AMENDMENT 14
Citizenship and civil rights protected

AMENDMENT 15
Voting rights for freedmen

AMENDMENT 16
Income tax permitted

SUPREME COURT DECISION
Miranda v. Arizona ruling

AMENDMENT 18
Prohibition of liquor

AMENDMENT 19
Woman suffrage

AMENDMENT 20
Terms of president and Congress

AMENDMENT 21
Prohibition repealed

AMENDMENT 22
Two-term limit for president

AMENDMENT 23
Voting in Washington, D.C.

AMENDMENT 24
Poll tax abolished

AMENDMENT 25
President disability rules

AMENDMENT 26
Voting age lowered to 18

AMENDMENT 27
Limits Congressional pay

Case Studies

NOTE TO TEACHER

The following exercises are designed to be copied and handed out to students. They can be used as the basis for class discussion or essays.

Each activity describes a case that either has gone before the Supreme Court or is similar to cases the court accepts. Instruct your students to review the cases and the arguments raised by the questions. Then tell your students to pretend that they are Supreme Court justices. You may have them debate the cases in class, basing their arguments on the Constitution. Or you may ask your students to write their arguments and opinions in essay form.

Some teachers may want to give their students the cases only and have the students make their own arguments from the facts of the case. Because of this, we have printed each case separately from the arguments.

Case One — Rap Singing and the First Amendment

THE QUESTION

Did a rap singer's agreement when he was paroled from prison violate his First Amendment rights?

The Case

California gangsta rapper Shawn Thomas, who performs under the name C-Bo, was sent to prison for illegally firing a gun. The crime occurred while he and others were giving an informal concert in a public park. When a fight broke out, Mr. Thomas fired a gun to get the fighters' attention. Then others in the crowd also fired shots, and one of these shots killed a man. For his reckless use of a weapon, the Mr. Thomas was arrested and sentenced to prison.

He was released on parole after serving nine months of a two-year sentence. As a condition of his parole, he agreed "not to engage in any behavior that promotes the gang lifestyle, criminal behavior and/or violence against law enforcement." He also agreed not to associate with any gang members. Similar limits are placed on most ex-convicts. Within months after his release, the rap singer made an album that included songs California authorities say violated his parole agreement. Among other things, the songs suggested that a local probation officer, sheriff, and district attorney be murdered. The songs referred to these individuals by name.

After the album was released, Mr. Thomas was arrested. Law enforcement officers say they had the right to arrest the singer because he broke his parole agreement. But Mr. Thomas and his supporters say the First Amendment guarantees freedom of speech. They argue that he should not have been arrested for simply saying, or in this case singing, something.

Case One — continued

ARGUMENTS FOR SHAWN THOMAS

The First Amendment gives Mr. Thomas an absolute right to use whatever lyrics he wants. His songs tell about the lives and treatment of African Americans and describe how blacks feel about this treatment. Mr. Thomas says that his lyrics include exaggerations, as do many works of art. The lyrics are not meant to encourage actual violence but to shock people and make them think about things that should be changed.

Rappers should not be sent to jail for their music. There are all sorts of songs about violence and outlaws. The writers and singers of those songs are not jailed because of their lyrics.

Giving up freedom of speech should never have been a condition of Mr. Thomas's parole. Freedom of speech is a fundamental First Amendment right. Giving up this freedom is not usually a condition placed on people who are released on parole.

ARGUMENTS AGAINST SHAWN THOMAS

Mr. Thomas was released on parole based on his agreement not to encourage gangs, crime, or violence against the police. He signed a pledge agreeing to these conditions. The lyrics on C-Bo's album were a violation of his parole agreement. He had not completed his two-year prison sentence, and he was only released from prison due to the good graces of the parole board. If he wants to be out of prison early, he has to live by the rules of the agreement he signed.

Free speech is a right many people have. But because of his conviction, Mr. Thomas has lost many other rights that other citizens have. For example, he can't vote or own a gun. Therefore, he would not necessarily still have the right to free speech.

The right to free speech doesn't mean you have the right to use your speech to do harm. Justice Oliver Wendell Holmes's "clear and present danger" rule could also be applied to these lyrics. According to this rule, people can be punished for writing or saying things if it can be clearly proven that their words could cause serious harm. For example, your right to free speech isn't protected if you yell "Fire!" in a crowded theater, unless there really is a fire. Mr. Thomas's songs do more than use words that some people think are offensive and insulting. The songs encourage people to do real harm. And they even name the people that he thinks should be harmed.

HOW WOULD YOU VOTE?

Was Mr. Thomas's right to free speech violated? Was he required to give up his right to free speech as part of his parole? If so, is it legal to make him give up his First Amendment rights, under the Constitution? Or were officials right to arrest him for what he said on his album? Were the terms of his parole fair? Did he violate his parole, and should he be sent back to prison?

Study the **First Amendment**. Then write your opinion on a separate sheet of paper. Be sure to back your opinion with arguments based on the Constitution.

 **Bible Studies in Schools**

THE QUESTION

Does an elective Bible study class in a public school violate the First Amendment clause separating church and state?

The Case

Parents in a school district in Florida wanted a course on the Bible to be taught in the high school. The school board received a petition with more than 1,200 signatures asking for the course. The class was to be an elective course — that is, students could choose to take it or not. The school district would pay for course materials and the teacher's training and salary and provide a room for the class, as it does for other courses. About 150 of the district's 13,000 students signed up for the Bible study class.

The district formed a committee to determine exactly what would be taught in this course and what might be left out. The committee, which consisted of 12 Christian and two Jewish members, decided the Bible would be taught as history, but that certain parts would be left out. These parts include accounts of miracles. The Old Testament would be taught in this course; the New Testament would be excluded.

A typical class would be taught in this manner: the class of 20 or so students would break up into small groups. The groups would read the same story, but from different versions of the Bible. The groups would make timelines of the events in the story and note facts about the names of people and places. The groups would then compare notes and decide whether the Bible story was historical. The class would also discuss whether the story was well written in each version. The teacher would lead discussion and direct study about the meaning of the Bible stories and what else was happening when these stories were written.

Some courts have said that a Bible course could be taught in public school if it was under the supervision and control of the school board, if the teachers were hired and fired by the board in the same manner as all other teachers and were not asked about their religious beliefs or lack thereof, if the course was offered as an elective, and if nothing in the course tried to convince students that the material was true or false.

A lawsuit was filed to stop this Florida school district from including the Bible study course.

Case Two — continued

ARGUMENTS FOR THE BIBLE STUDY CLASS

The Bible is an important part of Western culture. Many references in American humor, history, literature, and art come from the Bible. The class could also teach morals.

"It certainly may be said that the Bible is worthy of study for its literary and historic qualities," U.S. Supreme Court Justice Thomas Clark wrote in a 1963 decision. He said Bible study may be acceptable in public education, depending on how the course was taught.

Not allowing Bible study is a form of censorship. Students have as much right to learn about the Bible as they do any other subject. Keeping the Bible course out of schools is anti-religious.

ARGUMENTS AGAINST THE BIBLE STUDY CLASS

The Bible is, first and foremost, a religious text and should not be taught in public schools. Teaching it in a school that is run with taxpayers' money falls under the "establishment of a religion" that the First Amendment forbids.

This class presents the Bible as "historical," and it offers only the Christian view of the Bible. If the Bible is taught in schools, then other religious texts must be given equal weight. This could mean that a large amount of a school's resources would go toward teaching classes related to religions.

By presenting the Bible as historical, the class teaches that the stories in the Bible are facts. Not everyone believes this, and these views don't have a place in public school.

If the Bible is taught as historical fact, it would contradict facts taught in other courses, such as science classes.

HOW WOULD YOU VOTE?

Is the Florida district's Bible study course an establishment of religion? Is forbidding this class a form of censorship? Should schools be allowed to have Bible study courses or not? If so, what limits should be placed on these courses?

Study the **First Amendment**. Then write your opinion on a separate sheet of paper. Be sure to back your opinion with arguments based on the Constitution.

Immunity for the President

THE QUESTION

Can the president be sued while in office for acts that are not related to his or her official duties?

The Case

Paula Corbin Jones, a former employee of the state of Arkansas, accused President Bill Clinton of making unwanted sexual advances in 1991, while he was governor of Arkansas. Mr. Clinton denied the accusation. In 1994, lawyers for Ms. Jones filed suit in federal district court in Little Rock, Arkansas, claiming that she was punished for rejecting Mr. Clinton's advances. They said she was denied job promotions and treated rudely by her employers. They also said the president's behavior caused Ms. Jones to suffer great emotional upset.

Lawyers for the president filed a motion in federal court in Little Rock saying that the president had immunity from lawsuits like this while in office. Immunity means that someone has protection or freedom from something. In this case, it means that President Clinton is protected from being sued for his private actions while he is president. A federal district court judge ruled that the lawsuit could not go to trial until after Mr. Clinton left office. The judge said the president should not have total immunity from civil suits, like this one. A civil lawsuit is one in which a person is sued for money by a private citizen. A person is not charged with a crime in a civil suit. However, the judge also said that a trial on this charge would take too much of the president's time. The case went to a federal appeals court, where a panel of three judges, ruling 2 to 1, overturned the lower court ruling. The appeals court said that President Clinton had no constitutional grounds for delaying the suit and that the suit could go forward while he was in office.

At this point, the lawyers for the president filed a Supreme Court appeal asking that the president be granted immunity and that the lawsuit be delayed until he left office.

Case Three — continued

ARGUMENTS FOR IMMUNITY

Article II of the Constitution makes a single person — the president — responsible for the actions of the executive branch in much the same way that the entire Congress is responsible for the actions of the legislative branch, or the entire federal court system is responsible for those of the judicial branch. For this reason, the president has more responsibility than any other single government official. President Clinton does not have the time to defend himself from civil lawsuits that, like this one, have nothing to do with his actions or responsibilities as president. Such cases are distractions from more important government matters.

In 1982, the Supreme Court ruled that a president had complete immunity from private civil suits for any action within the "outer perimeter" of his or her official duties. This means there are even things related to the president's office that he or she cannot be sued for.

A single judge should not have the power to make the president interrupt his or her work duties to defend a lawsuit like this one. The Constitution separated the government into three branches to prevent one branch of government from threatening the workings of another in major ways.

ARGUMENTS AGAINST IMMUNITY

The president, like other officials, is subject to the same laws that apply to all citizens. There has never been a case in which an official was granted immunity for his or her unofficial, personal actions. A delay in this trial will most likely hurt Ms. Jones's case. As time passes, witnesses may forget things or even die. Evidence can be lost.

If President Clinton is granted immunity from civil lawsuits while he is in office in this case, it sets a very bad precedent. A precedent is a decision that sets the standard for other decisions. Once a precedent is set, other courts will often rule the same way. If the president is allowed to delay this lawsuit, it could have a very bad effect on our justice system. Lawsuits that should be resolved quickly could be put off for years. What if, for example, the president owned land that contained poisonous chemicals? People living near the land would have to wait years before they could sue the president to get the site cleaned up and get money for their injuries.

If lawsuits brought against the president interfere with his or her public duties, then Congress should pass laws that give the president stronger protection.

HOW WOULD YOU VOTE?

Does the Constitution give presidents immunity from the type of lawsuit Ms. Jones brought against President Clinton? Should the Constitution provide this kind of protection? Do you think the Constitution must always be followed exactly as it was written to decide cases such as this one?

Study **Articles II** and **III** of the Constitution. Then write your opinion on a separate sheet of paper. Be sure to back your opinion with arguments based on the Constitution.

Case Four: The Line Item Veto

THE QUESTION

Does the president of the United States have the power to veto parts of certain bills passed by Congress?

The Case

In 1996, Congress passed the Line Item Veto Act. This law gives the president the power to cancel, or veto, individual budget items in tax and spending legislation. This is called the "line item" veto because in a budget each item is shown on a separate line. The president can veto a "line" in a budget bill within five days of signing the bill into law. Because the act requires Congress to say which budget items can be deleted and which cannot, the president does not have a completely free hand. When the president vetoes a budget item, the money saved must be used to reduce the deficit. Congress can reject the vetoes the president makes by passing a special bill. This special bill can, in turn, be vetoed by the president, and this veto can be overridden in the normal manner by a two-thirds vote in both the House and Senate.

The line item veto law means that the president is not required to accept or reject entire bills. If the president likes most of a bill but dislikes certain things in it, he or she can use the line item veto to get rid of those things. The line item veto is also a tool the president can use to trim spending.

The Supreme Court decided to hear a line item veto case that grew out of two separate lawsuits that were filed against President Bill Clinton over his use of the veto. One challenge was filed by local hospitals in New York City and two medical worker unions. They claimed they were harmed when the president deleted a measure that would have given New York State $2.6 billion in Medicaid payments. The Snake River Potato Growers, a farm cooperative in Idaho, brought the second lawsuit. The potato growers said they suffered when the president deleted a measure that gave owners of a food processing plant a special tax break if the plant owners sold their facility to the potato growers co-op. These two lawsuits were later combined into one.

A federal court found the line item veto unconstitutional based on this suit. President Clinton appealed the case to the Supreme Court. The Court must decide whether the line item veto violates Articles I and II of the Constitution, which provide for the separation of powers among the branches of government. Article I also explains how a bill becomes a law.

Case Four — continued

ARGUMENTS FOR THE LINE ITEM VETO

There is no real case here because neither of the parties to sue the president is directly affected by the line item veto. If anyone should sue, it should be the state of New York or the food processing facility.

The Supreme Court has said that Congress is free to delegate — that is, give or share — some powers to the executive branch. This is permitted as long as Congress supplies guidelines under which the president is supposed to act. The line item veto power is similar to power that Congress has given to federal agencies. As with the line item veto, Congress gives each agency rules to follow in making decisions and defines the limits of the agency's power.

The Line Item Veto Act honors the "presentation clause" of Article I in the Constitution. Under this act, the president first signs the entire bill into law. Only then can he or she cancel specific provisions in the bill, as long as Congress has not identified those provisions as ones that may not be vetoed. In the case of the line item veto, Congress is not surrendering its power to make laws. It is merely letting the president cancel spending on new projects or tax breaks that benefit few taxpayers.

The law applies to a fairly small group of budget bills. It requires that any cancellation must be used to reduce the budget deficit and that the vetoes may not hold up necessary government functions.

ARGUMENTS AGAINST THE LINE ITEM VETO

The potato farmers and hospitals were injured by an act that gives one person — the president — the power to edit tax and spending bills. The potato farmers said the loss of the tax break changed the terms of a purchase they were trying to make. One attorney for the New York City hospitals estimated that "billions" of dollars of Medicaid payments would have been passed on to the city if not for the line item veto.

The "presentation clause" of Article I says that in order to become a law, a bill must be passed by both houses of Congress and signed by the president or passed by two-thirds majorities of both houses of Congress to override the president's veto. The Constitution requires the president to approve or disapprove a law in its entirety. A provision or part of the bill can only be repealed, or canceled, by the passage of a new law under the same formula. When the president vetoes parts of a bill under this law, it's the same as creating a new bill. Creating legislation is the job of Congress, not the president.

HOW WOULD YOU VOTE?

Do the hospitals, medical worker unions, and potato growers have grounds for a lawsuit? Does the line item veto violate the separation of powers as required by the Constitution?

Study **Articles I, II,** and **III** of the Constitution. Then write your opinion on a separate sheet of paper. Be sure to back your opinion with arguments based on the Constitution.

Case Five: Selecting Art for NEA Funding

THE QUESTION
Does the NEA have the right to refuse to fund works it considers "indecent"?

The Case

The National Endowment for the Arts, or NEA, is a government program that provides money in the form of grants to artists and museums. A grant is simply money given for a specific purpose.

In the 1980s, the NEA came under fire from various groups for funding a few works of art that some people considered offensive or obscene. In 1990, Congress passed a law requiring that the NEA only fund art that met "general standards of decency." Karen Finley was one of several artists who claimed they lost an NEA grant in 1990 because of these decency standards.

Ms. Finley is a performance artist — that is, an artist who chants, sings, recites, dances, or uses his or her own body in some way to illustrate some theme or make a point. Ms. Finley has a master's degree in art and has performed in museums throughout the world. She lost her NEA grant because of a performance in which she smeared chocolate syrup on her nude body and chanted "God is death!" She says the performance was about the abuse of women.

Ms. Finley sued the NEA, and two lower courts threw out the decency standards, calling the standards "vague." The government appealed the case to the Supreme Court. The issue before the court is not only whether Ms. Finley should get to keep her grant, but whether Congress exceeded its constitutional bounds in setting decency standards on the art it funds.

Case Five — continued

ARGUMENTS FOR THE NEA DECENCY STANDARDS

While decency standards may be one factor in choosing who or what gets a grant, they are not the only factor. The government has to be selective in what it funds or supports. The NEA gets hundreds of funding requests every year and grants, perhaps, two out of seven of them. Clearly, not everyone who submits a request is going to get a grant.

The government is not violating the Constitution by only funding some works of art any more than it violates the Constitution when it chooses the art it wants to put in its own buildings.

The NEA is not censoring or restricting the creation of art. The art community can produce whatever it likes, but it cannot expect public money to be used for work that might be considered obscene or that might offend the public. If people want to support these works of art, they have the right to do so on their own. Ms. Finley and other artists have no constitutional right to get money from the government for their work.

ARGUMENTS AGAINST THE NEA DECENCY STANDARDS

Ms. Finley's performance is not obscene. She has used nudity in her work, but nudity has been used in art and the theater for thousands of years.

The government can choose not to fund the arts if it wants. But if it does give money, it should not limit the way that art is expressed. To do this is a form of censorship. Artwork is meant to challenge the way people look at the world. Some forms of art have always been disturbing. Works that were considered outside mainstream values at the time they were created include Michelangelo's *Last Judgment* and Auguste Rodin's *The Kiss*. The NEA should give artists grants based on merit, not morality.

A decency requirement such as the one in this law is far too vague. No two people have the same standards or the same set of values. What one person considers obscene might be seen by someone else as perfectly acceptable. The NEA should not restrict its funding only to art that appeals to the greatest number of people. The government funds public works as such as highways, and city bus systems receive subsidies as well, even though not everybody uses these things.

Great civilizations place a high value on free speech and new ideas. Art is often an expression of these ideas. And great civilizations have always funded artists.

HOW WOULD YOU VOTE?

Can the government, like any other buyer, apply its own sense of taste to what it pays for? Or does the Constitution require that the government never place judgments on citizens' freedom of expression, even if federal funds are involved?

Study the **First Amendment**. Then write your opinion on a separate sheet of paper. Be sure to back your opinion with arguments based on the Constitution.

Case Six — Roe v. Wade

THE QUESTION

Does a state have the right to prevent a woman from getting an abortion?

The Case

Jane Roe was a single woman living in Dallas County, Texas, when she became pregnant. Jane Roe was not her real name, but it was the name used in this court case. Ms. Roe wished to end her pregnancy by an abortion performed by a licensed physician under safe conditions in a medical clinic. An abortion is an operation that removes a fetus from a pregnant woman's body. Under Texas law, a woman could not get an abortion unless her pregnancy appeared to threaten her life. Although a woman who got an illegal abortion was not charged with a crime, the physician who performed the operation was charged and could be punished.

Ms. Roe was unable to get a legal abortion in Texas and she could not afford to travel to another state for the operation. She claimed that the Texas statutes, or laws, that forbade doctors from performing abortions were unconstitutional. But Texas courts upheld the state's abortion laws. Her case against Henry Wade, the district attorney of Dallas County, went to the Supreme Court.

Case Six — continued

ARGUMENTS FOR ALLOWING ABORTION

It is the right of single women and married persons to choose when and if they want to have children. A state does not have the right to interfere in this decision. Although there is no stated "right to privacy" in the Constitution, the Fifth and 14th Amendments guarantee no person can be "deprived of life, liberty, or property, without due process of law." The 14th Amendment also says no state can make a law that takes away the rights of citizens. These amendments add up to a constitutional right to privacy. The Ninth Amendment says citizens have rights that aren't spelled out in the Constitution. Just because there is no stated right to privacy in the Constitution doesn't mean it doesn't exist.

American citizens are persons who are born in the United States or who are granted citizenship. A fetus is not a citizen or a person because it has not been born. Fetuses are not counted in population totals. Therefore, a fetus has no rights under the law.

Texas law about abortion is vague. In Texas, abortions that are necessary to save the life of a woman are legal. In these cases, the fetus is not considered to have the same rights as the woman. If abortion is legal some of the time, there is no reason it should not always be legal.

ARGUMENTS AGAINST ABORTION

There is no right to privacy spelled out in the Constitution. The protection of liberty in the Fifth and 14th Amendments is not broad enough to cover the right to an abortion when the mother's life is not in danger. Ms. Roe's right to privacy is not at issue here. An abortion is not a private matter: it includes not only the woman but also her doctor and the medical clinic.

The life of a fetus deserves state protection. A fetus begins to develop human features and organs very early. The state has the right to make laws about medical operations. Abortion is not the only operation that can be performed only under certain conditions. For example, a person cannot ask a doctor to cut off an arm or leg without a good reason.

HOW WOULD YOU VOTE?

Is a fetus protected under the Constitution? Does the Constitution contain an implied right to privacy — that is, one that is assumed, even if it's not spelled out?

Study the **Fifth, Ninth,** and **14th Amendments**. Then write your opinion on a separate sheet of paper. Be sure to back your opinion with arguments based on the Constitution.

Case Seven: Drug Testing in School

THE QUESTION

Does random drug testing of high school athletes violate the reasonable search and seizure clause of the Fourth Amendment?

The Case

The Vernonia School District of Vernonia, Oregon, operates one high school and three grade schools. Until the middle 1980s, the small town had never had much illegal drug use, especially among its young people. But around this time, teachers, the principal, and other people who run the school observed that high school students appeared to be using illegal drugs. Discipline problems increased greatly in the high school. Some students openly boasted that there was nothing the school could do about their drug use.

The school staff found that student athletes were among the leaders of the drug culture. This caused the district's administrators particular concern because drug use increases the risk of sports-related injury. At first, the district tried to deal with the drug problem by offering special classes and speakers. When none of these things solved the problem, Vernonia district officials began considering a drug-testing program. They held a parent "input night," and all the parents attending approved a student-athlete drug testing policy. The school board approved the policy and scheduled it to go into effect in all the schools in the district.

The student-athlete drug policy applies to all students participating in sports. Students who wish to play sports must sign a form consenting to the testing and obtain the written consent of their parents. Athletes are tested at the beginning of their sport's season. In addition, once a week during the season, the names of the athletes are placed in a "pool," and a student, with the supervision of two adults, blindly draws the names of 10 percent of the athletes for random drug testing. Those selected are tested that same day, if possible.

A student who is being tested first completes a form giving information about his or her health and any prescription drugs he or she takes. Then the student is required to produce a urine sample in the presence (although out of sight) of an adult monitor. The monitor checks the sample for evidence of tampering, and the urine is tested for drugs. Only a few members of the school district's staff ever learn the results of these tests, and the results are destroyed after one year. If a student test shows drug use, the student is tested again. If the second test is also positive, then school officials meet with the student and the student's parents. The student is given the choice of participating in a drug prevention program or not playing sports.

ARGUMENTS FOR DRUG TESTING

It is not unreasonable to expect public schoolchildren to submit to drug tests. They have to submit to physical examinations and be vaccinated to be admitted to school in the first place.

The privacy of student athletes is not violated by the monitoring of urine collection. Athletes dress and undress in front of each other. They are subject to physical exams and to special rules regulating their conduct. In this case, the collection process is similar to the conditions usually found in a public restroom.

Schools must do all they can to keep schoolchildren from using drugs. And it is even more important to stop drug use by athletes, for whom the risk of physical harm is high.

Only one set of parents objected to having their child tested for drugs.

The drug test is random and doesn't single out any student athletes.

ARGUMENTS AGAINST DRUG TESTING

Students are not criminals who must give up all their rights when they walk through the school door.

Under the Vernonia drug testing policy, any and all student athletes may be tested. But this does not make the policy "reasonable." A search is unreasonable if the person searched is not under suspicion of any wrongdoing. The policy calls for random searching of students who have not necessarily been suspected of drug use.

Collecting and testing urine is a type of personal search that violates the Fourth Amendment. Courts have already found that even scraping dirt from under a person's fingernails violates this amendment.

The school could determine drug use by other means.

HOW WOULD YOU VOTE?

Do you think the use of random drug testing in schools is a "reasonable search"? Is the privacy of students violated by the urine collection drug test method used by the school?

Study the **Fourth Amendment**. Then write your opinion on a separate sheet of paper. Be sure to back your opinion with arguments based on the Constitution.

Case Eight

Affirmative Action in Universities

THE QUESTION

Can public universities use race as a basis for accepting or rejecting students?

The Case

The University of California-Davis School of Medicine opened its doors in 1968. That year, 50 students attended. The only minority students in the first class were three Asian Americans. Over the next two years, university officials developed a program to increase the enrollment of minority students in the medical school. As part of this program, they set aside eight spots to be filled by minority students. In 1971, the size of the entering class was increased to 100 students, with 16 places set aside for minority students.

Each year, many more students apply to the UC-Davis medical school than are admitted. Candidates with overall grade point averages below 2.5 on a scale of 4.0 are rejected immediately. Members of the admissions committee then interview about one of every six remaining candidates. Students are admitted to the medical school based on these interviews as well as their grades, test scores, letters of recommendation, and backgrounds.

The special admissions program that was set up to fill the slots reserved for minority students operates with a separate admissions committee. Most of the people on this committee are members of minority groups. The candidates for the 16 special slots are interviewed and held to the same standards as the rest of the applicants, but they do not have to have a grade point average of at least 2.5.

Allan Bakke is a white male who applied to the Davis medical school in 1973 and 1974. In both years, Mr. Bakke's application was considered under the general admissions program, and he received an interview. He was rejected both times, although openings set aside for minority students were unfilled. Mr. Bakke had a higher grade point average and scored higher on tests and personal interviews than did most of the students admitted under the special program. After his second rejection, Mr. Bakke filed a lawsuit. He said the medical school had no right to reject him on the basis of his race. The California court agreed, but it did not order that he be admitted to the medical school.

Mr. Bakke appealed the decision, asking a higher court to require the medical school to admit him. The University of California appealed the ruling that its special admissions program was unlawful. The case of *University of California v. Bakke* eventually went to the Supreme Court.

Case Eight — continued

ARGUMENTS FOR THE SPECIAL ADMISSIONS PROGRAM

The 14th Amendment was written to grant equal protection to African Americans under the law. The Congress that passed the 14th Amendment is the same Congress that created laws that benefited only blacks.

Government programs often give preferences to one group over another. The government has programs that benefit veterans' groups and the disabled. Federal and state governments award a certain percentage of contracts to businesses owned by minorities.

Universities often give special consideration to the children of their graduates, the children of rich donors, and athletes. Why shouldn't universities be able to use race as grounds for admitting students or for giving some students special consideration? Selection of students is the job of university officials, not of the courts.

The university benefits by having students of different races and backgrounds. Students learn more about the world by being exposed to people who are different from themselves. Programs such as the one at the University of California are necessary to integrate the medical profession and increase the number of minority doctors.

ARGUMENTS AGAINST THE SPECIAL ADMISSIONS PROGRAM

The law states that no person shall, on the grounds of race or color, be kept from participating in any program that receives federal money. The University of California gets government money. The government and its institutions cannot give privileges to one person at the expense of another person. Disadvantaged people of all races should be given special consideration. But no applicant may be legally rejected because of his or her race in favor of another who is less qualified. Giving preferences to certain groups makes it appear that members of those groups can't succeed without special help.

It is true that schools in the United States are doing many things to end segregation. School children, for example, are bused to schools so that no schools in an area have all white students or all black students. But Mr. Bakke's situation is not like that. The University of California did not arrange for him to attend a different medical school in order to desegregate Davis Medical School; instead, it denied him admission and may have kept him from getting a medical education altogether.

HOW WOULD YOU VOTE?

Was the University of California-Davis, medical school right or wrong to set aside places for minority students?

Study the **14th Amendment**. Then write your opinion on a separate sheet of paper. Be sure to back your opinion with arguments based on the Constitution.

Case Nine: United States v. Richard Nixon

THE QUESTION

Can the president, because of his or her high office, keep any and all information he or she chooses from the courts?

The Case

On June 17, 1972, police arrested five men who were caught breaking into Democratic headquarters in Washington, D.C. The Democratic headquarters office was in the Watergate complex, and the scandal caused by this break-in came to be known as the Watergate affair. Investigators learned that the burglars were employees of President Nixon's re-election committee.

Republican President Richard Nixon was re-elected in November of 1972. The investigation of the Watergate break-in continued after the election. It soon appeared that not only the Committee to Re-elect the President, but possibly the president himself, was somehow involved in the crime.

In the summer of 1973 during a Senate investigation of the Watergate affair, one witness revealed that the White House had secretly tape recorded many of the president's conversations. A special prosecutor (a lawyer working for the government to take action against high government officials suspected of a crime) ordered that the tapes be given to investigators. President Nixon refused to give up the tapes. The special prosecutor and the Senate committee investigating Watergate filed petitions in U.S. district court to get the tapes. The district judge decided to review the tapes himself and ordered the president to give him the tapes. President Nixon appealed the order, but his appeal was denied. Eventually, the White House released edited transcripts of the tapes, but investigators still wanted the original recordings.

In 1974, the case of the *United States v. Nixon* reached the Supreme Court. The justices were asked to decide if the president had executive privilege in this case. Executive privilege is the right of the president to refuse to give to Congress or the courts certain communications that come from within the executive branch of the government. The president can withhold this information if it is found that keeping the information secret is in the best interests of the nation.

Case Nine — continued

ARGUMENTS FOR EXECUTIVE PRIVILEGE

A president and those who work with him or her must be free to discuss all possible solutions to a problem. They will not be able to do this if everything they say can be made public. The president's communications cover a wide range of secret material. He or she must discuss military operations and our nation's relations with other nations. It is important to our national interest that these communications are not made public. Therefore, the president has a greater need than other citizens to keep his or her communications private.

This case is between the president and the special prosecutor, who was appointed by the attorney general — a member of the president's cabinet and part of the executive branch of the government. The president has power over the special prosecutor; the prosecutor cannot make demands of the president. The dispute over the presidential tapes is a matter that should be settled within the executive branch. The courts should not even be involved in it.

ARGUMENTS AGAINST EXECUTIVE PRIVILEGE

Our nation has an "adversary system" of criminal justice. An adversary system is a system in which two parties argue against each other in a court of law. For this system to work, all the facts of a case need to be presented. The court cannot make a fair decision if some of the information is hidden. There are times when evidence can be kept private: for example, no person can be forced to be a witness against her or himself. But that doesn't apply to this case.

President Nixon says he has a privilege against revealing private or secret communications. The president did not say the tapes contain military information or secrets about U.S. relations with other countries. The special prosecutor isn't asking for any information that has to do with the security of the nation. And President Nixon hasn't given any special reason for executive privilege to be used in this case. All he is saying is that, in general, his conversations should be kept private. The United States government is divided into three branches. But these branches do not work independently, and each has some power over the others. This is what keeps one branch of government from getting too powerful or overstepping its limits. If a president had absolute executive privilege, he would never have to answer to the judicial branch.

It is true that the attorney general appointed the special prosecutor with the approval of the president. But only a certain group of congressmembers can fire the special prosecutor. The president does not have power over the special prosecutor.

HOW WOULD YOU VOTE?

Should the president always be able to withhold information from a court of law? Or should the president be made to follow the same rules as other people who are accused of crimes?

Study **Articles I, II,** and **III** of the Constitution. Then write your opinion on a separate sheet of paper. Be sure to back your opinion with arguments based on the Constitution.

Case Ten: The Gun Control Debate

THE QUESTION

Do communities have the right to ban firearms of any kind?

The Case

In 1981, John W. Hinckley Jr. attempted to assassinate President Ronald Reagan. He wounded the president and three other people, including Mr. Reagan's press secretary, James S. Brady. The assassination attempt opened up the ongoing debate about gun control laws — laws that limit the types of guns available or make it harder to get guns. Soon after the shooting, members of Congress urged the president to support stricter laws on the purchase of firearms. But President Reagan remained opposed to gun control.

James Brady was disabled by his wound, and he strongly supported creating tougher gun laws. After he was shot, Mr. Brady and his wife devoted their lives to working for laws that would keep guns out of the hands of criminals. Eventually their efforts resulted in the passage of the Brady Bill. This bill requires that a person who buys a gun must wait five days before he or she can get the gun. This waiting period is designed to give police time to look into the backgrounds of gun buyers and make sure they aren't criminals.

Other communities have enacted even stronger gun control measures. At least one town in Illinois has banned ownership of all handguns. Another made it illegal to buy, sell, or transfer any firearms. But people who are against gun control laws have said that these measures are too strict and that they violate the Second Amendment.

Case Ten — continued

ARGUMENTS FOR GUN CONTROL

Communities have the right to regulate things that have to do with public safety. For example, some states have banned the sale of fireworks. It is perfectly legal for communities to have their own gun control laws.

Banning ownership of firearms — especially of handguns — makes these weapons less available to citizens, but it also makes it harder for criminals to get them. When there are fewer guns available, violent crime goes down. Countries with the strictest gun control laws also have the lowest rates of death from firearms.

The Second Amendment says, "A well-regulated Militia, being necessary to the security of a free State, the right of the People to keep and bear Arms, shall not be infringed." The amendment refers only to a militia, or a small, local army. It does not give individual citizens the right to bear arms — that is, to own and use guns.

ARGUMENTS AGAINST GUN CONTROL

Many people own handguns to protect themselves against criminals. The handgun is like insurance. Criminals are less likely to attack someone who is armed or to enter a house when the owner is at home and has a gun.

Banning ownership of firearms will not stop criminals from obtaining them. Gun control laws will prevent law-abiding citizens from owning guns, but criminals will still be armed.

The term "militia," as used in the Second Amendment, refers to all citizens, who, during the Revolutionary War were armed and ready to defend their country and their freedom with their own firearms. The framers of the Constitution wanted to protect that right and that ability. They included the Second Amendment to insure that each individual American had the right to bear arms.

HOW WOULD YOU VOTE?

Can the government put limits, as the Brady Bill does, on people's ability to buy a gun? Do states or communities have the right to ban any and/or all firearms? Does the Second Amendment say that bearing arms is the right of every American? What role, if any, should the government play in gun control?

Study the **Second Amendment**. Then write your opinion on a separate sheet of paper. Be sure to back your opinion with arguments based on the Constitution.

Case 11: Gregg v. Georgia

THE QUESTION
Is the death penalty "cruel and unusual punishment"?

The Case

Troy Gregg and a companion, Floyd Allen, were hitchhiking on November 21, 1973, when they were picked up in a car by Fred Simmons and Bob Moore, both of whom were drunk. The car broke down and Mr. Simmons bought a new one using money from a large roll of cash. In Gwinnett County, Georgia, Troy Gregg shot and killed Mr. Simmons and Mr. Moore. Three days later, Troy Gregg and Floyd Allen were arrested in North Carolina. They had the car Mr. Simmons had purchased, and Mr. Gregg also had the gun that had killed the two men and money taken from Mr. Simmons.

Mr. Gregg admitted to police that he had killed the two men, robbed them of $400, and taken their car. At trial, Mr. Gregg said he had killed the men in self defense. The jury found Mr. Gregg guilty of two counts of murder and two counts of robbery.

Georgia, like many states, has a "bifurcated" trial system. This means that a jury decides the guilt or innocence of a defendant in one trial. Then, if a defendant is found guilty, he or she is sentenced after a second trial. There are several reasons for this system. One is that a defendant's background may have nothing to do with the crime he or she is being tried for but might make a difference in how harsh a sentence he or she is given. Another reason is that, although how a crime was committed may have nothing to do with a person's guilt or innocence, it may make a big difference in terms of the sentence he or she gets. In order for a person who is found guilty of murder to receive a death sentence in Georgia, there must be other events related to the murder that make it an especially bad crime. For example, the death penalty might be imposed if the criminal acted in a vicious manner or killed someone while committing another serious crime. At the second, sentencing trial, lawyers will bring in information about a person's background or about the specific events of the murder to try to convince the jury that the criminal should get a harsher or a lighter sentence. The judge tells the jury what evidence it can use to make its decision about the criminal's sentence.

Georgia adopted the bifurcated trial system after the 1972 case of *Furman v. Georgia*. In that case, the Supreme Court decided that the death penalty, as it was used in Georgia, was unconstitutional, based on the Eighth Amendment, which forbids "cruel and unusual

Case 11 — continued

The Case — continued

punishment." In *Furman,* the court said that criminals were often sentenced to death in a random manner and that juries were not well-informed about what information they should use to decide a sentence. The court ruled that the death penalty, as it was being handed down at that time, was "cruel and unusual" in the same way that being struck by lightning is cruel and unusual: in both cases, the court said, there was no reason that one person was affected when another was not. Georgia's bifurcated system was put in place to provide guidelines for when the death penalty should be imposed and to make sure juries understand those guidelines. The system was supposed to stop juries from sentencing criminals to death randomly.

The jury gave Mr. Gregg the death penalty after his sentencing trial. Mr. Gregg appealed his sentence, and in *Gregg v. Georgia,* the Supreme Court was asked to decide again if the death penalty was cruel and unusual punishment.

Case 11 — continued

ARGUMENTS FOR THE DEATH PENALTY

There are many safeguards to insure that only guilty people are sentenced to death. In order to convict a person of murder, a jury must be certain beyond a reasonable doubt that he or she is guilty. And the convicted person has every chance to appeal his or her death sentence.

Murder is the most extreme of crimes, and it deserves the most extreme punishment. But even a murder conviction is not enough for a death sentence. In order for someone to receive the death penalty, the crime must be especially horrible or the convicted person must have a history of committing similar crimes. The framers of the Constitution did not consider the death penalty to be unconstitutional. The Constitution refers to "capital" crimes — that is, crimes for which the penalty is death. The framers only wanted to be sure that a person was not deprived of life without due process of law; in other words, they wanted to make sure everyone had a fair trial.

ARGUMENTS AGAINST THE DEATH PENALTY

The Supreme Court in *Furman* ruled that the death penalty was cruel and unusual punishment because it was imposed randomly. The bifurcated trial system doesn't fix this problem. The death penalty will always be imposed randomly or unfairly. It is not possible for the justice system to develop a fair standard to decide who deserves the death penalty. Most states have laws that a criminal must commit a vicious and outrageous murder to be sentenced to death. But different juries will have different ideas about what is vicious or outrageous.

The death penalty is unfair because it falls heaviest on the poor and the powerless who cannot afford the best lawyers or defend themselves well.

Even after a prisoner is sentenced to death, there is always a question about whether he or she deserves to die. Prisoners stay on death row for years while their cases are being appealed, delayed, and retried. This is expensive for taxpayers and cruel for the criminals, who must live with uncertainty.

There is always the chance that a person who is innocent could be executed. People have been found innocent and released from prison after spending years on death row.

Even the worst criminal is still a human being, and it is wrong for the states to kill people.

HOW WOULD YOU VOTE?

Is the death penalty unconstitutional? Is it unconstitutional as it is applied in our court system? Should criminals ever be sentenced to death?

Study the **Eighth** and **14th Amendments**. Then write your opinion on a separate sheet of paper. Be sure to back your opinion with arguments based on the Constitution.

Case 12: Bilingual Education

THE QUESTION

Is a school district that does not have bilingual education violating the civil rights of non-English-speaking students?

The Case

The San Francisco, California, school system was integrated in 1971 as a result of a federal court order. In this case, "integrated" means that students of all races went to the same schools. In the past, students of different races had been kept apart. At that time there were 2,856 students of Chinese ancestry who did not speak English in the school system. Of those who spoke only Chinese, about 1,000 were given extra courses in the English language. About 1,800 of these students, however, did not receive any special instruction in English.

Non-English-speaking Chinese students brought suit against officials of the San Francisco Unified School District. The students asked that they be given equal opportunities to get an education. They did not say exactly what they wanted the school district to do, but they expected that all the schools in the district should provide some form of bilingual education. Teaching English to the non-English-speaking Chinese students was one choice. Teaching classes to this group in Chinese was another.

The district court decided against the Chinese students. The court of appeals agreed, saying that there was no violation of the "equal protection clause" of the 14th Amendment or of the Civil Rights Act of 1964. The "equal protection clause" says that everyone has equal rights under the law, and no state can deny a person those rights. The Civil Rights Act bans discrimination — that is, treating someone differently from others — based "on the ground of race, color, or national origin" in "any program or activity receiving federal financial assistance." All public schools receive some federal money. In 1973, the case went before the Supreme Court.

Case 12 — continued

ARGUMENTS FOR BILINGUAL EDUCATION

Under the law, school systems are responsible for making sure that students of every race, color, and national origin have the same opportunity to get an education.

Merely providing all students with the same facilities, textbooks, teachers, and courses is not treating the students equally if some of the students do not understand English and can't participate fully or learn in class.

The California school system demands that students understand English, but it does not ensure that all its students are given the instruction and the tools they need to meet this requirement.

ARGUMENTS AGAINST BILINGUAL EDUCATION

This is a public school system in California. The California Education Code states that "English shall be the basic language of instruction in all schools." That section allows a school district to determine "when and under what circumstances instruction may be given bilingually." It's up to the school districts to make choices about whether to use bilingual instruction.

There have been many cases in which the San Francisco school district has not given any special help to non-English-speaking students. But the school district hasn't purposely discriminated against them. It is not the district's fault that these students do not speak English. Nor is the district trying to prevent the students from learning English.

It's not fair to hire Chinese-speaking teachers to satisfy one group of students unless foreign-language speaking teachers are hired for every student or group that doesn't speak English. It could be expensive and maybe even impossible to find teachers who speak Polish, Hungarian, or any one of a number of other languages that students might speak.

HOW WOULD YOU VOTE?

Under what circumstances do you think schools should be required to provide bilingual education?

Study the **14th** and **15th Amendments**. Then write your opinion on a separate sheet of paper. Be sure to back your opinion with arguments based on the Constitution.

Case 13 — Income Tax

THE QUESTION
Can a person avoid paying income taxes if he or she believes such taxes are unconstitutional?

The Case

John L. Cheek was a pilot for American Airlines. For the years 1973 through 1979, he filed tax returns. After that, he stopped. Mr. Cheek also claimed an increasing number of withholding allowances from his paycheck — eventually claiming 60 by mid-1980. When money is withheld from a paycheck, it means that it is taken out before a person receives his or her pay. For example, some state and federal taxes are withheld, along with Social Security taxes. When a person claims a withholding allowance, he or she states a reason that less tax should be withheld from his or her paycheck. For the years from 1981 to 1984, Mr. Cheek claimed that he was exempt from — in other words, that he didn't have to pay — federal income taxes. In 1983, he unsuccessfully tried to get a refund of all taxes withheld by his employer in 1982.

Mr. Cheek was indicted for ten violations of federal tax law for willfully failing to file federal income tax returns and for trying to get out of paying taxes by claiming too many exemptions and allowances. The tax offenses with which Mr. Cheek was charged are "specific intent" crimes. These crimes require proof that a defendant knew he or she was breaking the law and that he or she acted intentionally, or on purpose. It must be proven that the defendant acted intentionally because the tax laws are very complicated, and it is easy for taxpayers to make honest mistakes that are not really crimes.

At Mr. Cheek's trial, evidence showed that he had been one of several parties in at least four civil cases that challenged the federal income tax system. In all four of those cases, the courts told the plaintiffs that many of their arguments were ridiculous or had been rejected by other courts.

Mr. Cheek admitted that he had not filed personal income tax returns during the years in question. He testified that, as early as 1978, he had begun attending classes and meetings sponsored by a group that believes the federal tax system is unconstitutional. Some of the speakers at these meetings were lawyers who claimed to give professional opinions about federal income tax laws. Mr. Cheek's defense was that, based on the information he received from this group and his own research, he honestly believed that the tax laws were unconstitutional and that his actions after 1979 were lawful. He said he believed that the wages he earned at his job were not "income" as defined in the 16th Amendment. He argued that because of this, he had not willfully disobeyed the law and should not be found guilty. Mr. Cheek was found guilty and he took his case to the Supreme Court.

Case 13 — continued

ARGUMENTS FOR PAYING INCOME TAXES

The courts had informed Mr. Cheek many times that he must pay income taxes and that, in the past, courts have rejected the idea that personal income taxes are unconstitutional.

The federal income tax system was established in 1913. It has been around so long that every American should be aware of it.

Even if Mr. Cheek did not understand everything about the tax system, there is a long-held rule in the American legal system that ignorance of the law or a mistake of law is no excuse for wrongdoing, nor is it a defense in court.

The 16th Amendment plainly states that Congress has the power to "lay and collect taxes on incomes, from whatever source derived." This amendment was ratified by the states.

ARGUMENTS AGAINST PAYING INCOME TAXES

The Fifth Amendment says that private property cannot be taken for public use without just compensation, or payment. Mr. Cheek did not feel he was compensated for the money taken from him in the form of taxes.

Filing tax returns is a form of self-incrimination. Self-incrimination is when a person says or does something that could lead to him or her being suspected or convicted of a crime. The Fifth Amendment protects people against self-incrimination. When Mr. Cheek filed tax returns, he was showing the government how much he had earned and how much he was or was not paying in taxes.

The 16th Amendment is unconstitutional because it goes against other parts of the Constitution, namely, Article I, which says taxes can be collected but says nothing about income taxes, and the Fifth Amendment.

HOW WOULD YOU VOTE?

Did Mr. Cheek willfully commit a crime? Is the income tax unconstitutional? Do you think the 16th Amendment could be challenged successfully in court?

Study **Article I** and the **Fifth, Sixth,** and **16th Amendments**. Then write your opinion on a separate sheet of paper. Be sure to back your opinion with arguments based on the Constitution.

Case 14: The Right to Trial by a Fair and Impartial Jury

THE QUESTION

Can a jury that has access to all true and untrue news reports and opinions about a trial come to a fair decision?

The Case

Marilyn Sheppard was killed in her Cleveland, Ohio, home during the early morning of July 4, 1954. On July 30, police arrested her husband, Dr. Sam Sheppard, for the murder. He went to trial in October and was found guilty on December 21, 1954.

When he was questioned by police and at his trial, Dr. Sheppard told the following story: On the evening of July 3, he and his wife had entertained neighborhood friends at their home. After dinner, they watched television in the living room. Dr. Sheppard dozed off on a couch. The next thing he remembered was hearing his wife cry out in the early morning hours. He hurried upstairs and in the dim light from the hall saw a "form" standing next to his wife's bed. The person attacked him, and Dr. Sheppard lost consciousness. When he came to, he took his wife's pulse and could not find any. He checked on his small son and found that the boy was all right. Dr. Sheppard then saw a person running from the house. He followed the person and they fought outside. Dr. Sheppard passed out again. When he regained consciousness he went into the house and called his neighbors. The neighbors came to the Sheppard house and found Dr. Sheppard slumped in a chair and his dead wife upstairs. They notified the police.

On July 7, the day of Marilyn Sheppard's funeral, a newspaper story ran in which the assistant county attorney — who was later the main prosecutor of Dr. Sheppard — sharply criticized Sheppard's family for not allowing him to be questioned right away. After this, news stories repeatedly reported that Dr. Sheppard would not cooperate with the police and other officials. This was not true — Dr. Sheppard had been interviewed by law enforcement officials several times.

On July 23, county law enforcement officials began an inquest into the crime. An inquest is an official investigation hearing about a death by local government and law enforcement officials. Inquests are used to decide if a case should go to trial. Dr. Sheppard's inquest was held in a school gym, and reporters from newspapers, television, and radio attended. The hearing was broadcast live.

Before and during the actual trial, the press continued to cover the Sheppard murder in great detail. The media often reported rumors and opinions as though they were true. They also reported information about the Sheppards' personal lives, including the fact that the Sheppards had an unhappy marriage and that Dr. Sheppard had been unfaithful to his wife.

Case 14 — continued

The Case — continued

Twenty-five days before jury selection began, 75 people were called as possible jurors. Cleveland newspapers published their names and addresses. All the prospective jurors received anonymous letters and telephone calls, as well as calls from friends, about the upcoming Sheppard trial.

In the courtroom in which the trial was held, a table was set up near the front of the room for the press. The first row of seats in the room was occupied by reporters from television and radio stations, and the second and third rows were reserved for reporters from out-of-town newspapers and magazines. Representatives of the news media also used all the rooms on the courtroom floor. A radio station used the room next to the jury room to make newscasts throughout the trial.

All of these arrangements with the news media and the media's massive coverage continued during the entire nine weeks of the trial. The courtroom remained filled to capacity with newspeople. Their movement in and out of the courtroom often caused so much confusion that, despite the loud speaker system set up in the courtroom, it was difficult for the witnesses and attorneys to be heard. Reporters were clustered near the defendant's table, which made private talk between Dr. Sheppard and his attorney impossible during the trial. They often had to leave the courtroom to get privacy.

The jurors themselves were constantly exposed to the news media. Before they were chosen, every juror except one testified that he or she had read about the case in the Cleveland papers or had heard broadcasts about it. During the trial, the judge suggested that jurors not read newspaper reports about the case or listen to broadcasts about it, but he did nothing to prevent them from doing so.

The jury found Sam Sheppard guilty of the murder of his wife, and he appealed. He had been in prison for 12 years when the case went before the Supreme Court. The court was asked to decide whether he had gotten a fair trial and whether the guilty verdict should be reversed.

Case 14 — continued

ARGUMENTS FOR REVERSING THE VERDICT

The jurors should have been kept from hearing the news reports of this trial. There is no way that they were not influenced or affected by these reports, and some of the reports were based on incorrect statements, rumors, opinions, or evidence that would not stand up in court. For a defendant to receive a fair trial, the jury's verdict must be based only on evidence presented in open court, not on reports and opinions from outside sources.

A defendant — especially one whose life is at stake — should be tried in a calm and solemn setting, not in a noisy room that resembles a circus and where he or she cannot even speak privately with his or her attorney.

The judge had lost control of this courtroom. He could not even stop the newspeople from disrupting the trial. No one could have a fair trial under these conditions.

The First Amendment guarantee of freedom of the press doesn't mean that the media is allowed to report rumors, untruths, and opinions as facts.

ARGUMENTS AGAINST REVERSING THE VERDICT

There is a great deal of evidence that Sam Sheppard committed this crime, and the jury found him guilty based on this evidence. His account of his actions during and after the crime were suspicious. He and his wife had an unhappy marriage. He had had affairs with other women. That these facts were reported in the newspaper did not make them less true.

The jury was made up of responsible citizens. The court had confidence that they would take their job seriously and not be influenced by news reports.

The press has a duty to report newsworthy events and keep the public informed. The court did not feel it had the power to keep the news media from reporting on the trial as it saw fit. This would violate the First Amendment right to freedom of the press.

HOW WOULD YOU VOTE?

Do you think Sam Sheppard received a fair trial?

Study the **First, Sixth** and **14th Amendments**. Then write your opinion on a separate sheet of paper. Be sure to back your opinion with arguments based on the Constitution.

Lawsuits Against States

THE QUESTION

Does the 11th Amendment prevent Congress from letting Indian tribes file lawsuits against states?

The Case

The United States has set aside many pieces of land as Indian reservations. Native American tribes own this land and, in general, run it. These reservations are governed by the federal government and the tribes. The states the reservations are in do not have authority over them. As a way to make money, many tribes have gambling operations on their reservations. Not all states want the tribes to have gambling. In 1987, the Supreme Court ruled that states cannot ban gambling on Indian reservations if the same gambling is allowed elsewhere in those states. Soon after, Congress passed the Indian Gaming Regulatory Act — IGRA — to control on-reservation gambling.

The IGRA allows some kinds of gambling on reservations. But other types of gambling are only allowed if they have been approved by tribal law and the National Indian Gaming Commission (a federal government agency) and if the tribe and the state have reached a contract, or formal agreement, about the gambling. The IGRA says that if the state and the tribe cannot come to an agreement, the tribe may seek the secretary of the interior's help. The secretary is supposed to assign a person called a mediator to help the tribe and the state work out their differences. The tribe and the state must seriously try to work out an agreement. This is called "negotiating in good faith." The mediator can make recommendations for how to solve the problem. If the state refuses to accept any of the mediator's recommendations, the secretary of interior can allow the tribe to have gambling based on the recommendations. The IGRA also states that a tribe can sue a state if the state does not negotiate in good faith.

In 1991, the Seminole Tribe and the state of Florida could not come to an agreement over the types of gambling that would be allowed on the Seminole reservation. The tribe said the state would not enter into good faith negotiations. The Seminole tribe sued Florida and its governor. Florida argued that the 11th Amendment says a state cannot be sued without its consent by citizens of the United States or any foreign country. Attorneys for the tribe said that Florida was breaking a federal law, the IGRA. This act, passed by Congress, allowed Indian tribes to bring lawsuits against states.

When the case reached the Supreme Court, the justices were asked to decide if Congress has the power, through the IGRA, to override the states' 11th Amendment immunity.

Case 15 — continued

ARGUMENTS FOR THE LAWSUIT

To protect their rights, citizens must be allowed to sue states in some cases.

The federal government is responsible for protecting Indian tribes and guaranteeing their rights. To do this, Congress can make laws requiring certain things of the states. If the states do not obey these laws, the states may be sued. The 11th Amendment does not protect states from federal laws.

The idea that a sovereign, or ruler, has immunity of this type comes from old English common law. This is law that is not written down, but agreed upon by custom and habits. The United States does not follow all of English common law, especially the idea that the sovereign, who in England was the king, can do no wrong. The United States was founded on the idea that the supreme power in the nation is the people, not a king or the state.

ARGUMENTS AGAINST THE LAWSUIT

The IGRA provides solutions for settling differences other than going to court. The secretary of the interior can allow on-reservation Class III gambling without the agreement of the state. Therefore, it is unnecessary for tribes to sue states.

States had protection from being sued when they were still independent, before they agreed to joing together to form the United States. The states did not give up all control over their affairs to Congress and the federal government when they became part of one nation; in particular, the states did not agree to be sued by private parties in federal court.

Just because Congress passed a law that Indian tribes can sue states does not mean this law is constitutional. Congress cannot change the Constitution by simply writing a new law.

HOW WOULD YOU VOTE?

Does the Seminole tribe have the right to take its case against Florida to court? Can Congress force Florida to negotiate with the tribe?

Study **Articles I** and **III** and the **10th** and **11th Amendments**. Then write your opinion on a separate sheet of paper. Be sure to back your opinion with arguments based on the Constitution.

Case 16: Trial by Jury in a Civil Case

THE QUESTION
Does a person always have the right to a trial by jury in a civil case?

The Case

In 1949, the owners of the trademark "Dairy Queen" signed an agreement with Mr. Wood to let him use the trademark. A trademark is a mark or brand name put on products to identify them as being made by a certain company. Mr. Wood had the right to open Dairy Queen restaurants or sell other people the right to open Dairy Queen restaurants in certain parts of Pennsylvania. For the right to use the Dairy Queen trademark, Mr. Wood promised to pay $150,000 to the trademark as owners. Under the terms of his contract, Mr. Wood made a small first payment and agreed to make the rest of the payments at the rate of 50 percent of all the money he received from using the Dairy Queen trademark. The contract also called for small payments from Mr. Wood every year no matter how much he made from the trademark. In 1960, the trademark owners wrote Mr. Wood a letter saying he had broken the contract by not making some of his payments. They canceled the contract and told Mr. Wood he could no longer use the Dairy Queen trademark unless he paid the amount he owed immediately. Mr. Wood continued to use the Dairy Queen trademark, and the trademark owners sued him for "breach of contract." Breach of contract means that someone has failed, without any legal excuse, to live up to his or her part of a contract.

The trademark owners said Mr. Wood owed them more than $60,000. The owners asked that the court issue injunctions — or court orders — to stop Mr. Wood from using the trademark. The owners also asked that Mr. Wood give them a statement showing how much money he had made from the Dairy Queen trademark.

Mr. Wood denied that there had been any breach of contract. He then asked for his case to be tried in front of a jury.

Defendants in criminal cases are always entitled to a jury trial. But the district court denied Mr. Wood a trial by jury because *Dairy Queen v. Wood* was a civil case, not a criminal case. A civil case is a court case that is brought by one citizen or group against another. Unlike the defendant in a criminal case, the accused person in a civil case is not charged with a crime, and he or she can't be sent to jail. Instead, the person bringing the civil case accuses the other party of some kind of wrongdoing and usually wants the accused person to pay money to right the wrong. In the case of *Dairy Queen v. Wood*, the Supreme Court was asked to decide whether or not Mr. Wood was entitled to a jury trial.

Case 16— continued

ARGUMENTS FOR A JURY TRIAL

The Seventh Amendment says that in any case that involves more than $20, the "right of trial by jury shall be preserved." In this case, the owners of the Dairy Queen trademark haven't named an actual amount. Instead, they are asking for an accounting of what is owed them and then payment of that amount. This amount will not be known until Mr. Wood has given this accounting. But they also said that they thought Mr. Wood owed them more than $60,000. Whatever the amount, it was clearly more than $20. It is fair that Mr. Wood should get a trial by jury to determine the exact amount.

Mr. Wood claims he had an oral contract with Dairy Queen that changed his original contract. He has a right to have a jury decide exactly what his legal contract with Dairy Queen is.

ARGUMENTS AGAINST A JURY TRIAL

In this case, the trademark owners are only asking Mr. Wood to do what is fair and right. They are asking that Mr. Wood give them a statement of what he owes them, that he pay the amount he owes, and that he not use the Dairy Queen trademark. These are things he would be expected to do under the terms of the contract. Mr. Wood is not being tried for breaking a law, just for breaking a contract. The court does not have to decide whether Mr. Wood should be punished or what that punishment should be. There is no need for a jury trial if a defendant doesn't face any punishment.

HOW WOULD YOU VOTE?

Should cases such as *Dairy Queen v. Wood* be tried before juries? Did Mr. Wood have the right to a jury trial?

Study the **Seventh Amendment**. Then write your opinion on a separate sheet of paper. Be sure to back your opinion with arguments based on the Constitution.

Case 17 — Silkwood v. Kerr-McGee

THE QUESTION

Can a state court punish a power plant that is governed by a federal agency and follows federal rules?

The Case

In 1974, the Kerr-McGee company had a factory near Crescent, Oklahoma, known as the Cimarron plant. The plant made plutonium fuel pins for use in nuclear power plants. The Atomic Energy Act, which was passed by Congress, said that plants that dealt with any kind of nuclear material were under the control and should follow the rules of the Nuclear Regulatory Commission (NRC), a federal government agency.

Karen Silkwood worked in one of the Cimarron plant's laboratories. On November 5, 1974, she was grinding and polishing plutonium samples. Plutonium is a highly radioactive and dangerous material, and Ms. Silkwood was using the special glove boxes that were designed for the work she was doing. She followed the plant's safety rules, which required her to check her hands for contamination when she took them out of the glove box. "Contamination" in this case means that a person got some of the plutonium on him or herself. Plutonium can cause serious illnesses and even death. Ms. Silkwood discovered some contamination. A more complete check showed contamination on her left hand, right wrist, upper arm, neck, hair, and nostrils. She immediately went through a process called "decontamination," which cleaned the plutonium off of her. The next day, Ms. Silkwood arrived at the plant and did some paperwork in the laboratory. When she left the laboratory she was checked for contamination, and once again she had plutonium on her. She was decontaminated again. On the third day, she was checked when she arrived at the plant, and she was already contaminated.

Suspecting that the contamination had spread to areas outside the plant, Kerr-McGee sent a decontamination squad to go with Ms. Silkwood to her apartment. The squad found contamination in several rooms. The contamination level in Ms. Silkwood's apartment was high enough that many of her personal belongings had to be destroyed. Ms. Silkwood herself was sent to the Los Alamos Scientific Laboratory to find out how much contamination there was in her body organs. She returned to work on November 13. That night, she was killed in an unrelated car accident.

Case 17 — continued

The Case — continued

When Ms. Silkwood's body was examined after her death, it was found that the level of contamination in her body was far below the limit under federal law. Still, Bill Silkwood, Ms. Silkwood's father, sued Kerr-McGee. His lawsuit was based on Oklahoma state law. He wanted money, or damages, for the injuries and property loss that Ms. Silkwood had suffered because of the contamination. During the trial, one Kerr-McGee witness admitted that the company had lost more plutonium during the period in question than the rules allowed. However, no one could show how plutonium got into Ms. Silkwood's apartment since she had been decontaminated before she left the plant. There was also evidence that Kerr-McGee followed most federal regulations.

The jury returned a verdict in favor of Mr. Silkwood and awarded him $10.5 million. Ten million dollars of this amount was to be paid as "punitive damages" — that is, money that Kerr-McGee had to pay as punishment for doing something wrong.

Kerr-McGee asked for a new trial. The company claimed that since it had followed the federal rules set by the NRC it should not be punished under state law. A court of appeals agreed that Kerr-McGee was regulated, or governed, by federal law and said that since the company had not broken federal law, it should not have to pay punitive damages. The Supreme Court was asked to decide how much power a state has over a federally regulated plant.

Case 17 — continued

ARGUMENTS FOR PUNITIVE DAMAGES

Although Congress wants to encourage the building of nuclear plants for energy, it does not want the plants built at the expense of public safety. Whenever it can be shown that plants have been careless, they should be severely punished.

Congress did not provide any federal remedy, or solution, for persons hurt due to a nuclear plant's carelessness. Therefore, Congress must have expected that people who were hurt in this way would be able to use the state courts to get money and other payment for their injuries.

The NRC can fine and take the licenses from nuclear plants that do not follow federal rules. But the NRC has no rules that say a plant cannot also be forced to pay punitive damages in state court.

ARGUMENTS AGAINST PUNITIVE DAMAGES

No one ever proved how Karen Silkwood was contaminated. There is no proof that the contamination was Kerr-McGee's fault.

The $10 million damage award was more than ten times greater than the largest single fine that the NRC had ever imposed. Kerr-McGee was following the federal rules it was supposed to follow. And there is no proof that Ms. Silkwood suffered very much from the contamination. Punishing Kerr-McGee to this degree by forcing it to pay these huge damages is unfair — especially when there is no proof that the company did anything wrong.

The NRC is an agency that is made up of experts in the nuclear industry. But if this award stands, operators of nuclear facilities will no longer be able to rely on the NRC as the source for the rules and policies they should follow. Juries who do not know anything about nuclear energy and safety will be able to force these plants to pay huge sums of money in punitive damages and make plants change the way they operate. This isn't good for the industry and, ultimately, for the public.

HOW WOULD YOU VOTE?

Should a state jury be allowed to decide whether a federally regulated nuclear power plant has been careless? Does the Constitution give the states powers over federally regulated facilities?

Study the **Tenth Amendment**. Then write your opinion on a separate sheet of paper. Be sure to back your opinion with arguments based on the Constitution.

Patenting Living Things

THE QUESTION
Can living things be patented?

The Case

In 1972, Ananda Chakrabarty, a microbiologist, worked for the General Electric company. A microbiologist is a scientist who studies plant and animal forms, or organisms, that are so small they can only be seen through a microscope. Bacteria and protozoa are two kinds of microscopic organisms. Dr. Chakrabarty created and filed for a patent on a new kind of bacterium that could be used to clean up oil spills.

A patent is a grant made by the government to the creator of an invention that gives the inventor the sole right to make, use, and sell that product for a certain period of time. Congress has passed laws that say that "any new ... process, machine, manufacture, or composition of matter, or any ... improvement thereof ..." that is useful may be patented. Congress decided that anything that would occur in nature, such as a mineral or a mathematical formula, cannot be patented because these things are not man-made.

To create the new bacterium, Dr. Chakrabarty changed the genes in other kinds of bacteria. Genes are found in every living thing. They tell cells what to do or what form to take. Different kinds and combinations of genes are what make every living thing unique. Dr. Chakrabarty's new bacterium would not have occurred in nature; it could only be made in a laboratory. Dr. Chakrabarty applied for patents for the process he used to make the bacteria, for the mixture of straw and bacteria that would be spread on oil spills, and for the bacteria themselves.

The patent office said that Dr. Chakrabarty could patent the process for making the bacteria but could not patent the bacteria themselves. This decision was based on the grounds that microorganisms are "products of nature" and as living things cannot be patented under U.S. law.

Dr. Chakrabarty eventually took his case to the Court of Customs and Patent Appeals, which ruled that even though microorganisms such as this bacteria are alive, that did not matter under patent law. The court said that Dr. Chakrabarty's bacteria were simply a man-made invention. The U.S. Patent Office appealed to the Supreme Court. The court was asked to decide if living bacteria are a "manufacture" or "composition of matter" under patent law.

Case 18—continued

ARGUMENTS FOR THE PATENT

The patent office has issued patents for living organisms in the past. In 1873, the patent office granted Louis Pasteur a patent on "yeast, free from organic germs of disease, as an article of manufacture."

Congress is free to amend patent law so that organisms produced by changing genes cannot be patented. Congress could also pass a law that says living things may or may not be patented. But until Congress takes such action, the law does not say that man-made organisms cannot be patented.

Dr. Chakrabarty is asking for a patent on something that has been unknown before now and that he made by changing its parts. His creation would not have occurred naturally. Therefore his invention is a new product and is man-made. He can patent this invention under present U.S. law.

While some people may not approve of patenting living things, the patent office does not have the right to reject patents because people dislike or fear certain inventions.

ARGUMENTS AGAINST THE PATENT

The patent office assumed that living things could not be patented and agreed to grant patents on some plants and seeds only after Congress passed specific laws commanding it to do so. Congress did pass special laws in 1930 and 1970 that named the types of plants that could be patented. If new laws were needed to provide patent protection for the plants, a law is also necessary for bacteria.

Congress is better able than the courts to determine whether or not invented microorganisms are patentable. It is up to Congress to decide how to handle cases like this. Until it passes laws on the patenting of bacteria, the courts should reject Dr. Chakrabarty's case and others like it.

If people are able to patent living things, it will make scientists' work harder and more expensive. Researchers will have to be careful not to accidentally use patented materials or processes without paying fees for them. In order to keep the right to use an organism or process, scientists will feel that they must patent any new gene pattern, for example, long before they understand anything about it.

HOW WOULD YOU VOTE?

Does the fact that the bacteria are living prevent Dr. Chakrabarty from patenting them?

Study **Article I** of the Constitution. Then write your opinion on a separate sheet of paper. Be sure to back your opinion with arguments based on the Constitution.

School Newspapers and the First Amendment

THE QUESTION
How much control do school officials have over the contents of a high school newspaper?

The Case

The Journalism II class at Hazelwood East, a high school in St. Louis, Missouri, wrote and edited a student newspaper called the *Spectrum*. The newspaper was published every three weeks or so during the 1982-1983 school year. More than 4,500 copies of the newspaper were distributed during that year to students, school personnel, and members of the community. The Hazelwood board of education provided funds from its annual budget for the printing of the *Spectrum*. Sales of the newspaper also helped pay for it.

The policy at Hazelwood East was for the journalism teacher, who was the newspaper adviser, to submit page proofs of each *Spectrum* issue to Principal Robert Reynolds for his review before the newspaper was published. Page proofs are copies of the pages before they are printed. On May 10, the newspaper adviser delivered the proofs of the May 13 edition to Principal Reynolds, who objected to two of the articles scheduled to appear in that edition. One of the stories described three Hazelwood East students' experiences with pregnancy; the other discussed the impact of divorce on students at the school.

Mr. Reynolds was concerned that, although the pregnancy story used false names "to keep the identity of these girls a secret," the pregnant students would still be identified from the text of the story. He also believed that the article's references to sexual activity and birth control were not suitable for the younger students at the school.

In addition, Mr. Reynolds was concerned because a student identified by name in the divorce story had complained about her father. The principal believed that the student's parents should have been given the chance to defend themselves or that they should have been shown the article and agreed to its publication. He did not know that the newspaper adviser had removed the student's name from the final version of the article.

Mr. Reynolds wanted to take out these two articles, and he did not believe that the students would be able to replace them in time to get the paper printed before the end of the school year. So he took out the pages on which the stories on pregnancy and

149

Case 19 — continued

The Case — continued

divorce appeared. The removal of two pages meant that the newspaper was only four pages instead of six. It also meant that all the other stories on those two pages did not get printed. Mr. Reynolds told other school officials of his decision, and they agreed with him.

The student editors felt that their newspaper had been censored and their First Amendment rights had been violated. To censor something, such as a book or article, means to remove it, or remove parts of it, because you don't like what it says. The student editors took the case to district court. The court ruled that Principal Reynolds's concerns were reasonable. It also said that since he believed the students would not have time to redo the pages on which the stories appeared, it was reasonable for him to remove two full pages of the newspaper. The case went to the court of appeals, which found in favor of the students. This court decided that the *Spectrum* was a public forum — that is, a place for the students to discuss ideas and express themselves. As a result, the court ruled, school officials were not allowed to censor the newspaper's contents. The court also said that school officials should not have censored the articles unless their publication would cause the school to be sued or would somehow disrupt the school. The school district took the case to the Supreme Court and asked the Court to decide if school officials had control over the contents of the school newspaper.

Case 19 — continued

ARGUMENTS FOR THE STUDENT EDITORS

The principal did not have the right to censor articles unless the articles would have disrupted classwork or violated the rights of others to the point that the school would have been sued. There is no evidence that the articles removed would have done either of these things.

Even if the principal acted in a reasonable manner by removing the articles, he had no right to take out two whole pages of the newspaper.

The purpose of the student newspaper is to teach journalism to the students. Censoring the newspaper does not do this unless the school officials believe that students should be taught to never report bad news, express unpopular views, or print a thought that might upset the people who pay the bills.

In the past, the Supreme Court has ruled that students in the public schools do not "shed their constitutional rights to freedom of speech or expression at the schoolhouse gate." The Court has ruled in favor of freedom of expression in school even if states or local school districts disagreed with what was expressed. For example, a public school may not force a student to salute the flag.

ARGUMENTS AGAINST THE STUDENT EDITORS

The school district funded the newspaper and, therefore, school officials had control over what was printed in it. The district, in fact, could even have stopped publication of the newspaper.

Principal Reynolds was correct in removing the two pages. He honestly believed that the students did not have time to remake the pages or rewrite the articles. The articles would have embarrassed some students and their parents. And the student writers did not follow good journalism rules when they did not give the parents discussed in the divorce article a chance tell their side of the story.

Hazelwood East's school newspaper is a not a public forum. It is a tool for teaching students about journalism. From the beginning, students understand that their adviser and the principal had the right to censor, change, or take out their articles.

The First Amendment rights of students in the public schools are not the same as the rights of adults in other places. A school does not have to put up with student speech that does not agree with what the school is trying to teach.

HOW WOULD YOU VOTE?

Did the Hazelwood East principal have the right to take articles out of the student newspaper? What rights do students have to freedom of speech and expression at school?

Study the **First Amendment**. Then write your opinion on a separate sheet of paper. Be sure to back your opinion with arguments based on the Constitution.

Case 20 — International Whaling

THE QUESTION
Can conservation groups force the United States to punish other countries for killing whales?

The Case

In 1946, 15 nations formed the International Convention for the Regulation of Whaling (ICRW). The purpose of this organization was to limit the number of whales that were killed each year. The United States was a founding member of the ICRW; Japan joined in 1951. The ICRW set up a schedule that set limits on the number of whales that could be killed from various whale species. In addition, the ICRW established the International Whaling Commission (IWC), which had the power to change the whaling schedule and set new quotas for the number of whales that could be killed. A quota is some group's, or, in this case, some country's, share of a total amount. The quotas had to be followed by IWC members if they were accepted by a three-fourths majority vote. Under the terms of the Convention, however, the IWC had no power to impose sanctions, or punishments, for quota violations. Moreover, any member country could file an objection to a change in the schedule by the IWC. When it filed an objection, the nation was no longer bound by the quotas set by the whaling schedule.

Many Americans were upset that the IWC could not make its member nations obey whaling quotas. And Congress decided to pressure whaling countries to limit the number of whales they killed. In 1971, Congress passed the Pelly Amendment to the Fishermen's Protective Act. This amendment said that the U.S. secretary of commerce was to certify to the U.S. president if citizens of a foreign country were conducting fishing operations that could "diminish the effectiveness" of an international fishery conservation program. In this case, "certify" means to state that something actually happened. To "diminish the effectiveness" of something means to reduce its ability to work. For example, the effectiveness of whale conservation programs would be diminished if so many animals were taken that not enough whales remained to reproduce and replace those killed. The Pelly Amendment said that the president could decide whether or not to put sanctions on certified nations. Between 1971 and 1978, the secretary of commerce certified several nations, but the president chose not to put sanctions on them. In 1979, to strengthen the U.S. stand against nations that violated whaling quotas, Congress passed the Packwood Amendment to the Magnuson Fishery Conservation and Management Act. The Packwood Amendment said that if the secretary of commerce certifies a nation, the president must put sanctions on that nation. Sanctions might include not allowing citizens of the nation to fish in American waters and not allowing United States companies to buy fish from that nation.

Case 20 — continued

The Case — continued

In the early 1980s, the IWC said that certain types of sperm whales could not be killed at all, and it ordered whaling to be stopped for five years beginning in 1985. Japan did not want to follow these restrictions, and it filed objections to both limitations. However, in 1984, Japan and the United States came to an agreement in which Japan promised to stick to certain whaling limits and to stop whaling by 1988. In return for Japan's agreement to reduce and then stop whaling, the secretary of commerce promised that the United States would not certify Japan under either the Pelly Amendment or the Packwood Amendment. Shortly before this agreement took effect, several wildlife conservation groups filed suit in federal district court, seeking to make the secretary of commerce certify Japan. The court decided in favor of the wildlife groups, ruling that killing whales over the quotas set by the IWC diminished the effectiveness of the ICRW. The court ordered the secretary of commerce to immediately certify to the president that Japan was in violation of the sperm whale quota. An appeals court agreed. The Supreme Court was then asked to decide if, despite the agreement between the two countries, the secretary had to certify Japan and the U.S. had to impose sanctions against that nation.

Case 20 — continued

ARGUMENTS FOR CERTIFYING JAPAN

There is some argument that because this case involves an international agreement, a federal court in the United States cannot review it. This is not true. What the case really involves is whether a government official — the secretary of commerce — was doing his duty. It is a question of U.S. law.

The wildlife conservation groups had every right to bring this case to court. They can bring action to make a government agency perform its duty. To bring a case to court, the groups must prove that they suffered some injury or harm by the agency's failure to act. In this case, the members of the groups claimed that their activities, such as whale watching and the study of whales, would be affected if too many whales were killed.

The IWC has decided that a zero quota — that is, killing no whales — is needed to conserve whales. Since Japan continues to kill whales, it is clear that Japan is hurting the conservation program. Congress made the law that said the secretary of commerce must certify nations under certain conditions. If the secretary fails to do so, he is rewriting the law. It is not the job of a member of the executive branch of government to make laws.

ARGUMENTS AGAINST CERTIFYING JAPAN

The conservation groups can claim that reducing the number of whales does harm to their activities. But the Pelly and Packwood Amendments do not say that the United States must protect whale watching and the study of whales.

It is up to the secretary of commerce to decide that citizens of a foreign country are conducting fishing operations in a manner that "diminishes the effectiveness" of the ICRW. But the law does not say exactly what "diminish the effectiveness" means. The secretary — not the conservation groups or the courts — must decide at what point a nation deserves to be certified.

In passing the Pelly and Packwood Amendments, Congress's first goal was to protect and conserve whales and other endangered species. The secretary met these goals by entering into the agreement with Japan. Under this agreement, the United States did not put sanctions on Japan and Japan promised to stop whaling in the near future.

HOW WOULD YOU VOTE?

Did the secretary of commerce fail to fulfill his duty by not certifying Japan? Would an agreement between Japan and the United States be the best way to save the whales?

Study **Articles I, II,** and **III** of the Constitution. Then write your opinion on a separate sheet of paper. Be sure to back your opinion with arguments based on the Constitution.

Case 21: Seizing Property and Double Jeopardy

THE QUESTION
Can taking a person's property and sending him or her to jail for the same crime be considered double jeopardy?

The Case

Guy Jerome Ursery grew marijuana in a heavily wooded area not far from his home in Shiawassee County, Michigan. Believing that the marijuana plants were grown on Mr. Ursery's property, Michigan police officers got a warrant to search his house and yard. In the Ursery house, they found marijuana seeds, stems, and stalks. The police took, or seized, these items. There was no evidence that the Ursery family sold the marijuana to anyone else. But the federal government went to court in 1992 seeking forfeiture of Mr. Ursery's home and land because his property had been used in the drug trade. "Forfeiture" is when the government takes property without paying for it. Mr. Ursery agreed to pay a fine of $13,250 to keep the government from taking his property. In February of 1993, federal prosecutors charged Mr. Ursery with violating federal drug laws. He was tried, a jury found him guilty, and he was sentenced to 63 months in prison. After being convicted, Mr. Ursery claimed the government had put him in double jeopardy by trying him on criminal drug charges after he had already been punished in the property forfeiture action. Jeopardy is danger or risk.

The double jeopardy clause of the Fifth Amendment says, "nor shall any person be subject for the same offence to be twice put in jeopardy of life or limb." In past cases, the Supreme Court has ruled that this clause protects people from being tried and punished more than once for the same crime.

Mr. Ursery appealed his conviction, and the court of appeals agreed that the conviction on top of the forfeiture did violate the double jeopardy clause. Federal prosecutors argued that the forfeiture action was against Mr. Ursery's house, not against his person. The forfeiture was meant to stop, or deter, Mr. Ursery from using the house for drug trafficking. Prosecutors said that deterring someone from committing illegal acts is not the same as punishing him or her. The Supreme Court was asked to decide if Mr. Ursery had been punished twice for the same crime.

ARGUMENTS FOR BOTH THE FORFEITURE AND CONVICTION

The United States government must do everything it can to stop drug trafficking within this country. Seizing property in drug cases is an important tool in this effort. It does help deter crime when people no longer have a way to commit crimes.

The forfeiture case against Mr. Ursery was not a "jeopardy" because his life and limbs were not put in any danger by the seizure of his house.

If an owner misuses property so that it is dangerous in his or her hands, the property can and should be taken away from him or her. Using a property to grow, store, or sell drugs is illegal and dangerous.

Since the earliest years of this nation, Congress has allowed the government to take the property of and to punish a criminal for the same crime. For example, a smuggler could be sent to prison and made to forfeit his or her property.

ARGUMENTS AGAINST MR. URSERY'S CONVICTION

During prohibition, when it was illegal to manufacture and sell alcohol, distilleries — the places where alcohol was made — were seized by the government. However, all the houses where people stored and drank alcohol illegally were not seized; nor would this have been possible. It is not reasonable today to seize all the houses where marijuana is found. It is ridiculous to think that a person does not suffer when his or her house is taken from him or her. The forfeiture of Mr. Ursery's property can only be considered punishment.

The punishment in this case is far greater than the crime deserves. Mr. Ursery used his house to store marijuana, but he did not grow the plant on his property. He was not accused of selling marijuana. The forfeiture of a house because marijuana was found in it could be considered an excessive fine under the Constitution.

Property can be seized when it is somehow related to a crime. For example, if property had been used to commit a crime, if it is itself stolen, if property was purchased with stolen money, or if ownership of property is itself a crime, that property can be seized. The police took the marijuana seeds, stems, and stalks found on Mr. Ursery's property. He had no right to own them, and their seizure was not punishment. However, he did not buy his home with money earned from the sale of marijuana or from some other illegal activity. There was nothing illegal about his ownership of this house, and it should not have been seized.

HOW WOULD YOU VOTE?

Was it fair under the law to seize Mr. Ursery's house and then convict him for owning drugs?

Study the **Fourth, Fifth,** and **Eighth Amendments**. Write your opinion on a separate sheet of paper. Be sure to back your opinion with arguments based on the Constitution.

Supreme Court Decisions

Although some of the cases in this section were hypothetical, or made up, the cases are all based on actual situations, and many of them are real cases that were argued before the Supreme Court. The list that follows tells you how the justices ruled in each case. Did your decisions match those of the Supreme Court?

1. The case involving Mr. Thomas was resolved before it went to court. The county decided not to jail him for writing and singing rap songs that called for violence. Mr. Thomas, however, had violated his parole in other ways. He was jailed for these other parole violations.

2. The case about Bible studies courses in public schools is based on a real situation, but it has not been argued before the Supreme Court.

3. In *Clinton v. Jones*, the court ruled that the president did not have immunity from civil actions while still in office.

4. The court ruled that the Line Item Veto Act of 1996, which gave the president the power to cancel provisions of statutes he or she has signed into law, was unconstitutional. The court decided that the line item veto would allow the executive branch to make laws and that this was the job of the legislative branch — that is, Congress.

5. The court upheld a decency test for awarding federal grants in *NEA v. Karen Finley*. In the 8 to 1 decision, the court ruled that having this test did not violate the First Amendment.

6. In *Roe v. Wade*, the court decided that the state could not stop physicians from performing abortions during the first three months of pregnancy. After that, the state could regulate abortions.

7. The court ruled that the Vernonia school district had the right to randomly test student athletes for drugs.

8. In deciding *University of California Regents v. Bakke*, the court said the Davis Medical School should not have refused to admit Allan Bakke on the basis of race and ordered that he be admitted.

9. In *United States v. Nixon*, the court ruled that the president does not have unlimited, or absolute, privilege to withhold information needed for "due process of law."

10. This case has never been challenged in court.

Supreme Court Decisions — continued

11. In *Gregg v. Georgia*, the Supreme Court found that in extreme cases the death penalty is an appropriate punishment.

12. The Supreme Court ruled in *Lau v. Nichols* that schools must provide some sort of bilingual education for non-English-speaking students.

13. In *Cheek v. United States*, the court found that Mr. Cheek had to pay his income taxes and that he should have challenged the income tax laws in court instead of simply refusing to pay taxes.

14. Sam Sheppard was released from prison as a result of the court's decision in *Sheppard v. Maxwell*. The court found that he was not tried before an impartial jury.

15. The court upheld the 11th Amendment in *Seminole Tribe of Florida v. Florida* and ruled that the state could not be sued in this instance.

16. In *Dairy Queen v. Wood*, the court said that Mr. Wood had the right to a jury trial in a civil case.

17. In *Silkwood v. Kerr-McGee*, the court ruled that a state jury could award punitive damages — that is, money damages to punish the company — against a plant regulated by a federal agency.

18. The court decided that the bacterium was man made and could be patented in *Diamond v. Chakrabarty*.

19. In *Hazelwood School District v. Kuhlmeier*, the court decided that student newspapers can be censored by school authorities.

20. The court ruled that the secretary of commerce had the authority to decide when and if a nation should be certified. According to the decision in *Japan Whaling Association v. American Cetacean Society*, neither the Pelly Amendment nor the Packwood Amendment required the secretary to certify Japan for refusing to abide by the IWC whaling quotas.

21. In *United States v. Ursery*, the court said that convicting Mr. Ursery after the forfeiture action on his property was not double jeopardy.

Glossary

act — A formal legislative decision or law.

amendment — A change made to a document.

amicus curiae — Literally, "friend of the court." In Supreme Court cases, groups not directly involved in a case that may be affected by the case can file *amicus curiae* briefs.

Anti-Federalists — Group that favored a weak national government and strong state governments. They thought the biggest weakness in the original Constitution was the lack of a Bill of Rights to restrain the national government.

appellate court — An appeals court that hears cases previously heard in another court.

appeal — To take a case to a higher court for review.

appoint — To name or choose someone for an office or position.

apportionment — The allocation of legislative seats, in this case by population. Each state is apportioned seats in the House of Representatives according to its population.

argument — Oral presentation of a case made by an attorney before a court.

article — One of the seven parts of the Constitution that describe how the government is run.

Articles of Confederation — The first official charter of the United States, it was ratified by the 13 original states in 1781 and replaced by the Constitution in 1789. It gave some national governing authority to a Congress and treated each state much like a sovereign, or independent, nation.

autocracy — An absolute monarchy or totalitarian form of government.

bankruptcy — The state of being without money and having debts.

bifurcated trial policy — A two-tier trial system in which a jury first decides if a person is guilty or not guilty of a crime and then if the person is found guilty, meets again to decide the person's punishment. This policy has been used in capital punishment cases since 1976.

bill — A proposed law given to a lawmaking body for passage.

bill of attainder — A law enacted by a legislature to punish an individual without a trial in court.

Bill of Rights — The first ten amendments to the Constitution.

broad construction — The idea that the Constitution should be interpreted in a broad sense. Broad constructionists believe the Constitution should be flexible enough to address problems the framers of the Constitution could know nothing about.

Cabinet — A panel of the president's closest advisors.

capitation — In this case, a head tax.

calendar — A schedule that contains the names of bills or resolutions to be considered by House or Senate committees. In the Supreme Court, a list of cases to be heard during a session.

censure — In the Senate, the denunciation of a member because of an offense.

census — A count of the population done every 10 years to decide how many members of the House of Representatives each state will have.

checks and balances — Provisions in the Constitution that ensure that no one branch of government has dominance over the other two, and that each branch acts as a check on the others. The Constitution also gives states certain powers that can't be taken over by the federal government; thus, the states have a check on federal power. Likewise, the federal government has powers over the states. Establishing the system of checks and balances was one of the most important aims of the Constitution.

chief justice — The head of the Supreme Court, appointed by the president.

civil rights — The basic human rights enjoyed by citizens in a nation. Individual civil rights are described in the amendments to the Constitution.

clause — In this case, a phrase or set of words in an article or amendment.

cloture — A movement to end a filibuster. Three-fifths of the Senate must approve in order to end a filibuster.

committee — Sets of senators or House members who work on specific bills to present to Congress. Specific committees also recommend to Congress whether presidential appointments should be approved.

compromise — To find a middle course to an agreement.

concur — To agree. In the Supreme Court, a justice who agrees with a majority opinion on a case but does so for different reasons than the majority may write a concurring opinion.

confederation — An association of sovereign states.

Congress — The Senate and the House of Representatives.

constituent — A resident of a legislative district.

Constitution — The basic set of rules by which our nation is run.

convention — A meeting of a group of people with a specific purpose or goal to accomplish.

decision — The judgment made by a court when settling a case.

delegate — A representative for constituents in a legislature or convention.

democracy — System of government in which citizens elect their leaders.

dictatorship — Rule by one person who is usually unelected.

dissent — To disagree. In Supreme Court cases, a justice who disagrees with the majority opinion may write a dissenting opinion stating his or her objections.

double jeopardy — The term for being tried twice for the same crime.

due process of law — Protection against arbitrary denial of life, liberty, or property, as stated in the Fifth and 14th Amendments.

elastic clause — The clause in Article I, Section 8 of the Constitution that gives Congress the power to make all laws "necessary and proper" to carry out government business. Called the "elastic clause" because it gives Congress broad powers that aren't enumerated, or specifically stated, in the Constitution.

electoral college — The electors from the states who meet after the popular presidential election to cast ballots for president and vice president. When people cast their votes for president, they are actually voting for electors who are supposed to vote the way the people voted. The number of each state's electors is equal to the number of its representatives and senators.

Emancipation Proclamation — Proclamation by President Lincoln made in 1863 that freed slaves in Confederate states not yet occupied by Union armies. Because the proclamation did not extend to Union states, the 13th Amendment abolishing slavery in the nation was proposed and adopted.

enumerated powers — The powers of the executive, legislative, and judicial branches specifically written down in the Constitution.

ex post facto law — A law enacted to prosecute persons who committed an act when it was not a crime.

exclusionary rule — Rule that allows evidence illegally obtained in a criminal case, to be excluded from being presented in court. What evidence can be excluded under this rule has been the basis of a number of Supreme Court cases centering on the "illegal search and seizure" rule of the Fourth Amendment.

executive — The branch of government that carries out the laws made by the legislature. The chief executive of the United States is the president.

executive privilege — The right of the president to withhold confidential information from Congress and the courts. The Supreme Court has found that the president has some executive privilege, although it's not stated in the Constitution. However, the president does not have an absolute right to executive privilege.

extradition — The deportation of a person accused of a crime from one state to the state where the crime was committed.

federal — Pertaining to a system of government in which a number of states recognize a central authority or government while still retaining some authority of their own.

Federalists — Group that favored passage of the Constitution and a strong national government.

filibuster — A lengthy, non-stop speech designed to delay enactment of or votes on legislation.

government — The system by which a country or state is run.

Great Compromise — Agreement at the constitutional convention that led to the two parts of Congress, one with membership based on population, the other with a fixed number of members.

habeas corpus — Literally, "have the body." It means that people detained by the police have the right to appear in court and find out why they are being detained. No one can be detained for long without going before a judge to learn what he or she is charged with.

House of Representatives — One of the two parts of Congress, its members are elected every two years. The number of representatives from each state is based on the state's population.

impeachment — The accusation and trial of a high public official for misconduct in office.

implied powers — The powers of the executive, legislative, and judicial branches not specifically written down in the Constitution, but needed by these branches in order to carry out their enumerated duties. Debate over the extent of implied powers has been the source of numerous Supreme Court cases.

inauguration — The formal ceremony for the installation of a president.

incorporation doctrine — The idea that the Supreme Court can make the Bill of Rights apply not only to the national government, but to state governments as well. Most of the Bill of Rights has been incorporated by the Supreme Court to apply to states.

incumbent — The current occupant of an elected office.

joint resolution — A measure, similar to a bill, that must be approved in both parts of Congress and by the president.

judiciary — The branch of government that operates the courts of justice.

judicial review — The power of the courts to declare acts of the legislative and executive branches constitutional or unconstitutional.

jurisdiction — A word embracing every kind of legal action. In this case, it refers to the power to interpret or apply the law.

lame duck — An elected officeholder who will be leaving office either through the loss of an election or retirement.

law — In this case, a legislative act passed by both parts of Congress and signed by the president.

legislature — The branch of government that makes the laws.

lobbyists — Representatives of special interest groups or corporations who attempt to influence legislators in their votes.

monarchy — A governmental system in which a king or queen rules.

naturalization — The process of giving the rights and responsibilities of a citizen born in the United States to a non-citizen.

nullification — The declaration by a state or states that laws passed by Congress are unconstitutional. Nullification has been firmly discredited.

oath of office — the formal pledge or promise to carry on the duties of a government office honestly.

omnibus bill — a package of legislation that includes a variety of different proposals on one subject, such as crime or highways.

override — To try to reverse, or overturn, a presidential veto of legislation by means of a two-thirds majority vote in both houses of Congress.

patent — A grant made to a person by the government that says he or she invented something.

perjury — The crime of lying under oath.

platform — A statement of principles and objectives promoted by a party or candidate that is used to win the support of voters.

precedent — A court ruling that has a bearing on all legal decision in similar cases that follow.

pocket veto — Failure by the president to sign a bill passed by Congress into law in the 10 days before Congress adjourns.

poll tax — Also called a "head tax," a tax a person has to pay in order to vote. Banned by the 24th Amendment.

preamble — The opening statement of purpose in the Constitution.

president — The chief executive of the United States. He or she must be at least 35 years old, must be born a U.S. citizen, and a resident of the United States for 14 years.

president pro tempore — A senator elected by his or her peers to preside over Senate proceedings when the president of the Senate — the vice president — is absent.

quorum — the minimum number of members of a legislative chamber who must be present to do business. In the House 218 members constitute a quorum, while in the Senate 51 members is a quorum.

ratify — To approve or pass something.

ratification — Approval by a legislative body of agreements entered into with other states or constitutional amendment proposals.

repeal — To reverse or revoke something; the 21st Amendment repealed the 18th Amendment.

representative government — System of government in which people elect other people to represent them in government.

reserved powers — In the Tenth Amendment, the rights reserved for the states and not for the federal government.

roll-call vote — A vote in which all senators participate by answering "aye" or "nay" when their names are called.

secession — Withdrawl or separation from an organization. In 1860 and 1861, Southern states declared they had the right to secede, or withdraw, from the Union. They held that the United States was a contract among states from which a state could withdraw at any time. The Civil War followed.

Senate — One of the parts of Congress. There are two senators from each state, and senators serve six-year terms.

separation of powers — Constitutional division of power among the legislative, executive, and judicial branches. Along with establishing the system of checks and balances, establishing this division was the original purpose of the Constitution.

sovereignty — In a nation or state, the independent authority to make and carry out decisions.

strict construction — The idea that the Constitution should be read closely and that it should not be interpreted broadly.

suffrage — The right to vote.

term — length of time for which an elected official holds a political office. In the Supreme Court, the length of time the court meets in any year.

treason — The act of betraying one's country.

unalienable rights — Rights of individuals that cannot be transferred, or that one possesses forever.

veto — The right of a president to return a bill unsigned to Congress, with the result that the bill will not become a law.

whips — Party members elected by the Senate who assist the party leader by organizing legislative business.

writ — A written court order commanding the person who receives it to perform or not perform acts that it specifies.

BOSTON TEA PARTY